STEP-BY-STEP
TAPPING

STEP-BY-STEP
TAPPING

EFT – The amazing self-help technique
to heal mind and body

Sue Beer and Emma Roberts
EFT Masters

This book is dedicated to all our inspirational students and clients who have taught us so very much, thank you!

An Hachette UK Company
www.hachette.co.uk

First published in Great Britain in 2013 by Gaia, a division of
Octopus Publishing Group Ltd, Endeavour House,
189 Shaftesbury Avenue, London WC2H 8JY
www.octopusbooks.co.uk

Distributed in the US by Hachette Book Group USA, 237 Park Avenue,
New York NY 10017 USA

Distributed in Canada by, Canadian Manda Group, 165 Dufferin Street,
Toronto, Ontario, Canada M6K 3H6

ISBN 978 1 85675 328 9

A CIP catalogue record for this book is available from the British Library.

Printed and bound in China.

10 9 8 7 6 5 4 3 2 1

Disclaimer
The case studies in this book are based on actual clients. Some names and identifying
features or case details have been altered to protect their privacy.

While impressive results have been reported with EFT and other Energy Psychologies,
the field is still considered experimental. Given that, nothing in this book should be
construed as a promise of benefits or guarantee of any results.

This book represents the views and the opinions of the authors, who are not here
engaged in rendering medical, psychological, legal or other professional advice. The
reader therefore takes complete responsibility for his or her health and well-being.
This book is sold with the understanding that the authors and the publisher are not
rendering medical advice of any kind, nor is this book intended to replace medical
advice, nor to diagnose, prescribe or treat any disease, condition, illness or injury.

The ideas and information in this book are not intended as a substitute for medical
or psychological care. If you are under medical or psychological supervision, please
consult your healthcare professional before using the procedures described in this
book. The authors and publisher disclaim to any person or entity for any liability, loss
or damage caused or alleged to be caused incurred directly or indirectly as a result
of the use, application or interpretation of any of the contents of this book.

Contents

INTRODUCTION

'Emotional Freedom Techniques work by reconnecting your mind with your body's messages, restoring harmony where before stress and anxiety, or other unwanted feelings and negative states, may have prevailed.'

What is EFT?

This is a book that can change your life. Emotional Freedom Techniques (EFT) is self-help in a new way – it is not about ideas, theories or positive thinking, rather it is a simple, easy-to-learn practical tool that really works. By focusing your mind on problem areas while applying pressure with your fingertips to specific acupressure points on your body, you will discover how you can influence your physical and emotional well-being.

You will learn to reconnect your mind with your body's messages, restoring harmony where stress and anxiety or other unwanted feelings and negative states may have prevailed. Understanding that the remedy really can be in your own hands is very empowering.

Who can benefit from EFT and what can it do for you?

Anyone can benefit from learning EFT, from the very young to the aging. It is perfectly safe for children to learn for themselves and the same Tapping Sequences can soothe a toddler's rage or an elderly person's aches and pains. Once learned it will become a friend for life.

You can use EFT to help with a wide range of emotional and physical issues. EFT can help with stress and anxiety, physical pain, addictive cravings, confidence problems and painful memories. You will also learn how tapping in pairs can create intimacy and deepen the connection between two people.

It is a tool that teaches us we have more power over our own state of mind and therefore our health and happiness than we may have thought. These days many people are looking outside mainstream medicine for solutions. Using EFT to help with everyday stress and anxiety will help you take optimum benefit from whatever other treatments you may be receiving. In fact, EFT will work happily alongside medical and complementary approaches, and it is safe to use if you are taking medication.

Nowadays people from all walks of life are learning to empower themselves. We have reports of EFT successes from playgrounds to the highest offices in the land, from children to celebrities and sports stars. It started by word of mouth and now EFT is a radical tool for positive change, which is spreading fast. And fortunately the claims of its devotees are increasingly being backed up by research. EFT has been known to work when all else fails. There are numerous examples of the positive effects of tapping on a wide range of physical, psychological and emotional issues, as you will learn from the real-life case studies in this book.

The development of EFT

Gary Craig, the founder of EFT

Emotional Freedom Techniques (EFT) is the brainchild of American engineer and performance coach Gary Craig who has spent a lifetime being fascinated by how we can help ourselves lead healthier, more fulfilling and successful lives.

In the mid 1990s he became interested in the work of Dr Roger Callahan, an eminent psychotherapist, psychologist and academic, who in turn was curious about Eastern healing modalities and the concept of energy meridians. He had studied kinesiology and acupuncture alongside his mainstream psychotherapy practice.

In 1980, Dr Callahan was working with a patient, Mary, who had a severe water phobia and experienced frequent headaches and terrifying nightmares related to her fear of water. She had gone from therapist to therapist for years with no real improvement. Callahan had been working with her for a year and a half with only a slight change using conventional psychological techniques. One day, Mary complained of a stomach ache that seemed to come on when she thought about water. In a flash of inspiration, he decided to experiment by tapping underneath her eyes (the end point of the stomach meridian). To his astonishment, she immediately announced that her phobia was gone and she rushed down to his swimming pool and began splashing water on her face! The phobia had disappeared completely and never occurred again (Mary reported this herself when she was filmed 11 years later).

How did such a severe phobia disappear just like that? It would seem that when Mary was experiencing the fear, the energy flowing through her stomach meridian was disrupted, causing the stomach ache and that energy 'blockage' caused her emotional intensity. Tapping under her eye sent pulses of energy through the meridian, unblocking it and restored the flow. Once this energy meridian was returned to balance the emotional intensity – the fear – went away. Herein lies the most powerful thing you are ever likely to learn about your unwanted emotions: they are caused by energy disruptions.

Callahan continued to evolve Thought Field Therapy (TFT), a complex therapeutic technique that creates a series of different algorithms (tapping protocols or sequences) for any specific issue. We owe Dr Callahan an enormous debt of gratitude for his inspiration and dedication.

Inspired simplification

Gary Craig's inspired contribution was to offer a simplification of Dr Callahan's process. This is Emotional Freedom Techniques or EFT, which is easy for all to learn as the same tapping points are used whatever the issue.

Since Craig's innovation, EFT has continued to evolve and develop as therapists and practitioners from all schools incorporate these tools into their practices. While there are many variations of the basic technique used worldwide, we believe that the fundamentals of this

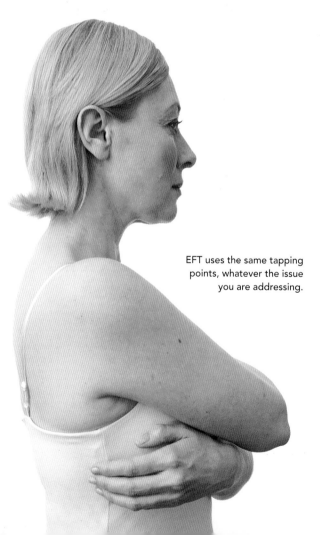

EFT uses the same tapping points, whatever the issue you are addressing.

technique, according to Gary's original concept, are the most effective and user-friendly way of creating change easily.

We have been fortunate enough to learn from the original master and, continuing in his spirit of generosity in sharing knowledge and experience, we have been able to pass on these breakthrough techniques to hundreds of individuals and groups around the world. Looking back, we could not have foreseen the positive changes that we ourselves were about to undergo when we first stumbled upon tapping over a decade ago. Our own lives have seen a rapid transformation. We've gone from quietly doing a good job as teachers and therapists, to appearing on a world stage alongside Gary Craig and other leaders in the field, and witnessing our own clients and students emerge and make their own contributions. This is emotional freedom – the freedom to express who you are, and fulfil your potential in your own special way. This book can show you the way, step by step.

We cannot emphasize enough the benefits of learning the basics really thoroughly. If you do, you will undoubtedly see positive results, and your own creativity and intuition will grow and will deepen your understanding. That has certainly been our own experience and has also led to one of our EFT innovations, the 'Heart Anchor'. The Heart Anchor is an amazingly powerful positive resource that you will learn to use alongside the tapping.

Welcome to these exciting times where more and more people are learning to clear their own emotional baggage, and create lives filled with hope and happiness – for themselves!

How EFT works

Emotional Freedom Techniques (EFT) works by rebalancing the body's energy system. Energy (called *Chi* or *Qi* in Chinese culture or *Prana* in Vedantic philosophy) flows around the body through a system of meridians that were mapped out by the Chinese over 2,000 years ago. Meridians are invisible channels through the body that carry energy to every organ and system. Although these energy pathways are not physical structures, meridians can be likened to the wiring of a house, or the veins and arteries through which blood flows.

Our body contains an intricate network of connective tissue, known as the cytoskeleton, which allows subtle energy to be transmitted throughout it. The cytoskeleton has a tree-like arrangement; the main branches are the meridians, and these divide into smaller branches, which eventually connect with our cells as tiny twigs. The EFT points we use are points of access into this cytoskeleton of connective tissue. They are points through which information flows freely back and forth between our body and the outside world.

In order to maintain optimal health our energy system needs to be balanced. We all go in and out of balance many times during every day, and often the energy system rights itself without our even knowing about it. When our energy flows freely through these meridians we experience health and happiness in our lives. We are 'in the flow'.

However, life happens, and at times most of us will experience some form of stress or trauma that blocks our energy from flowing freely. If left untreated, these blocks can result in 'dis-ease', either emotional or physical, or both.

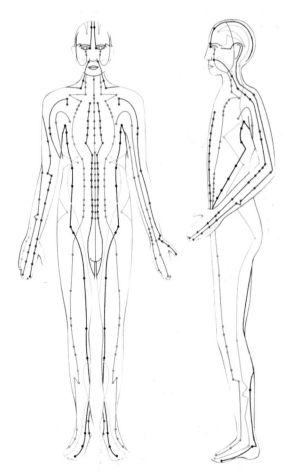

The meridian lines

Energy, by its very nature, is active. In health it flows freely around the body. When a blockage occurs the natural vitality and fluidity of the energy has nowhere to go, and it stagnates, causing dis-ease – a feeling of not being 100 per cent well or happy.

A non-invasive technique

EFT offers us a simple and easy way to clear these blockages, allowing the energy to flow freely again, restoring our path to optimal health and happiness. Sometimes this happens very quickly, in other instances we may need to be more specific, breaking down an issue into its component parts. We learn to become detectives and take charge of our own lives.

This non-invasive and safe technique works by applying gentle pressure (or tapping) to the end points of the meridians while we tune into specific negative thoughts, emotions, memories or physical discomforts. This tapping sends a vibration along these pathways, which in turn clears the blockage and brings us back into balance. As we tap, we name the problem we are addressing out loud, for example, 'fear of public speaking', which then guides our system to the specific issue we wish to treat.

One of the features of EFT is that it is actually not necessary to know which points relate to which organs in order to experience positive change. EFT works by tapping the same eight points regardless of the issue involved. Although there are points all over the body, the EFT points are all 'end points' of the meridians, which means that they are close to the surface of the skin and easy to stimulate with the fingertips.

EFT is not hypnosis, distraction or just positive thinking. The fact is that we do not yet know the exact mechanism by which it works, and await further research. We do know that EFT seems to create much greater communication between mind and body. When we are suffering from stress or problems of any kind we have often become disconnected from our emotions. We need our emotional responses to navigate and appreciate life. In fact, it is impossible to experience an emotion without feeling it on a physical level in the body – when we are cut off from bodily feelings we are cut off from life. Conversely, we can be terrorized by our feelings, living in a state of hyper-alertness. Tapping seems to create a state of 'mindfulness', a healthy emotional awareness and balance.

We are all the products of our history. We live our lives in the present according to the beliefs and experiences we have had along the way. While for some people these beliefs and life experiences are empowering and positive, for others they can be limiting and keep us stuck. When we apply EFT to our old hurts, fears, anxieties and resentments that still 'get' us today, we are able to let go of negative emotions and our limiting beliefs. We are then able to move forwards positively in our lives. And we know exactly what to do when we encounter the next block – the solution is literally at the end of our fingertips!

How to use this book

This book will guide you through the basics step by step to put you in charge of your health and happiness. Using clear, easy-to-understand and visually appealing instructions you will begin to experience the benefits as you learn.

Everything that you need to get started, along with the basic tapping points, can be learned in minutes. Then you can either go through the book chapter by chapter or, if you prefer, go straight to the chapters with the topics that interest you most. You will need to write things down as you go, and keep track of your progress, so we recommend you get yourself a special notebook for this purpose.

As your guides in this process we are not only EFT Masters but experienced therapists with more than 20 years in practice across a range of disciplines including psychotherapy, hypnotherapy, NLP and life coaching. We have a shared fascination for two things – discovering what works, and passing our knowledge and understanding on to others. EFT has transformed our own work with others in countless positive ways and we have been privileged to pass this amazing gift on to others through our teaching. This book brings together our deep understanding of how to use tapping techniques with our experience as teachers to allow anyone who is curious to discover the possibilities for themselves. It is written for everyone – for you! All you have to do is begin.

We have so many examples of people who have transformed their own lives – healing themselves from fears and phobias, physical pain, food cravings and so on – that what used to seem miraculous to us has almost become commonplace! If you are ready and willing this book will guide you through the process of successful change.

Write things down as you go in a notebook and keep track of your progress.

To get the most out of this book, there are a few things to bear in mind. Most importantly, be aware that you can't do anything wrong. The worst that can happen is that your tapping is temporarily ineffective and you need to refine your approach. Secondly, don't be put off if a feeling initially seems to get worse – if you keep tapping the intensity will subside. Lastly, consider working with a friend. It can be really helpful, as well as fun, to chart your progress together.

Chapter 1

HOW TO TAP

'Tapping is a gentle approach to clearing the energy blocks in the mind-body system that may be interrupting your healing processes, both physically and emotionally.'

Introducing 'tapping'

EFT is a very practical, hands-on (literally) approach to problem-solving. Also known as 'tapping', it is a gentle approach to clearing the energy blocks in the mind–body system that may be interrupting your healing processes, both physically and emotionally. The points we tap are the end points of the body's energy meridians, where they are closest to the surface of the skin.

In this book we will use nine tapping points, which comprise an easy-to-remember and apply routine, known as the 'Short Cut' version of EFT.

It is worth taking time to learn the Tapping Sequence thoroughly as described below so that you have it on automatic pilot.

Tapping is best learned in small building blocks, starting simply and building your confidence until you are able to experiment and become more flexible on your own. We suggest beginning by working with a problem where the results will be easy to measure, such as levels of anxiety or a physical symptom. So to begin the process of learning to tap, we will start by using the generic phrase 'this problem'. As you go along you will learn how to choose effectively the right words to describe the problem or problems specific to you.

There are two parts to the Tapping Sequence we use here, the first part is called the Set Up (see opposite) and the second is the Tapping Sequence (see pages 22–23).

The reason we use the sequence we do is merely that it is easy to remember as it works down the body, before ending on the Top of the Head point. The Top of the Head point, known as the Meeting of 100 Pathways in Chinese medicine, is a recent addition to the tapping protocol, following the recommendation of a number of acupuncturists, hence it being added to the end of the Tapping Sequence.

Unlike acupuncture, where the practitioner needs to be very precise when positioning their needles, with EFT there is more flexibility. As long as you are tapping in the general area you do not need to worry about being exactly on the point: we have met people who have been tapping in the 'wrong' places and still getting results – as the meridians flow all over the body it is actually very unlikely you will miss them.

Part 1 – The Set Up

The Set Up is the first part of the EFT Tapping Sequence. It is used to correct Psychological Reversal (PR), which is the energetic equivalent of self-sabotage and is caused by subconscious negative thought patterns and limiting beliefs. Once the Set Up has been done, we move on to the Tapping Sequence, tapping on eight different points.

We can get past PR by tapping on one point – the Karate Chop – while repeating our 'Set-Up Statement' three times. The Set-Up Statement is designed using language that states clearly the specific issue we are addressing alongside a positive affirmation. So you might say, for example: 'Even though I have this sadness/depression/anger, I deeply and completely love and accept myself.'

The generic affirmation used with EFT, and the one that we will use throughout this book, is 'I deeply and completely love and accept myself'. However, not everyone is able to say such a powerful statement initially. If this applies to you, feel free to alter the Set-Up Statement to one that feels more comfortable for you. Examples include: 'I am OK', 'I am good', 'I am cool', 'I am open to the possibility of loving and accepting myself' and 'I love and accept myself', or anything else that works for you as a positive self-affirmation. You do not have to believe it! Children might want to use a phrase such as 'I am cool' or 'I am a good kid'. Check it out with them and adjust your words to suit them.

The Set Up is a very important component of the tapping. It aligns the energy system in such a way that it can then respond to the rest of the tapping. Something powerful happens in our subconscious mind with the juxtaposition

of the negative ('I have this sadness') and the positive ('I completely love and accept myself') statements. The combination of acknowledging the specific problem and then welcoming the possibility of self-acceptance anyway allows our systems to begin to relax and get ready to respond to the tapping. It opens up the lines of communication.

Psychological Reversal

The Set Up is designed to counteract subconscious self-sabotage (referred to as Psychological Reversal or PR in Energy Psychology terms). PR comes and goes and there is no way of telling if it is there at any one time. However, if it is there, the tapping routine that follows (see pages 20–21) will not be effective, so just do the Set Up anyway; if PR is not there you will do no harm and it only takes a minute or so.

We are all familiar with the subconscious saboteur that is Psychological Reversal. It is the part of us that makes us eat chocolate cake when we are on a diet, the powerful part that can distract us from achieving our goals. Sometimes it is obvious, often it is more subtle and we are left with a sense of frustration at our seeming 'stuckness'. So addressing Psychological Reversal can be thought of as ensuring our batteries are aligned in the correct way so that when we press our buttons and apply the tapping it works smoothly.

Sometimes just saying a basic Set-Up Statement is not enough and you may find yourself blocked anyway – the tapping just seems to be getting nowhere. At these times you may need to be a little more creative with your Set-Up Statement, using words such as these:

- 'Even though I am frightened to get over this, I deeply and completely love and accept myself.'
- 'Even though I don't want to get over this, I deeply and completely love and accept myself.'
- 'Even though others don't want me to get over this, I deeply and completely love and accept myself.'

- 'Even though it is not safe for me to get over this, I deeply and completely love and accept myself.'

These blocks may not be in your conscious awareness, so just try out different statements and see what happens, even if they don't seem to make sense in the moment! We call these Primary Reversals, issues around safety, desire, fear and deserving, and they can keep us truly stuck until they are specifically addressed with the tapping.

To begin with, say the words aloud. This gives them more emphasis and makes the tapping more effective. The words direct the subconscious mind to the specific problem you want the tapping to address. However, if you are 'in' the problem before you begin to tap, and you are feeling panicky or tearful, for example, then don't worry about the words, just tap; you already have the attention of your subconscious mind and there is no need for direction.

The Karate Chop

When tapping the Set Up, use two fingers (usually your index and middle finger) on your dominant hand, and tap on the fleshy edge at the side of your other hand – the point you would use to deliver a karate chop. Use enough pressure so that you can feel it but are not hurting yourself – remember you are only sending a vibration of energy down that point. This spot is called the Karate Chop (see photograph, left).

The Karate Chop – use two fingers (usually your index and middle finger) on your dominant hand to tap on the side of your other hand on the spot where you would deliver a karate chop to someone.

As you tap on this point repeat your Set-Up Statement aloud three times: 'Even though I have [this problem], I deeply and completely love and accept myself.' The words 'this problem' appear in square brackets throughout the book to indicate that you need to fill in words to describe your own problem at this point, and direct that piece of the Set-Up Statement to your own specific issues.

The Sore Spot

There is an alternative way to correct Psychological Reversal and that is to use the Sore Spot while doing the Set Up. Locate the Sore Spot by placing your hand over the notch at the base of your throat, and moving it down slightly and then across slightly, either to the right or left (the Sore Spot is mirrored on both sides). You have found the Sore Spot (see photograph, right). Now, using the flat of your hand, rub on this area and repeat your chosen Set-Up Statement three times.

The Sore Spot is so named as it may be sore or sensitive for some people. This is because lymphatic congestion occurs there, and when you rub it with your hand you disperse that congestion. Using the Sore Spot when you do the Set Up is just as powerful as using the Karate Chop (KC), and you can use whichever you prefer. We refer to the Karate Chop in this book for simplicity's sake, but when we do so, you can substitute the Sore Spot.

Set Up recap

So in summary, the first part of EFT is the Set Up, which includes tapping on the Karate Chop (or rubbing the Sore Spot), while repeating your specific Set-Up Statement three times. While it may seem strange to say these words aloud, and you may not believe them (most people don't), just SAY THEM ANYWAY! If you are really struggling to do this, begin with 'I am OK' or 'I am good' or 'I am cool', but always with a view to working towards self-acceptance.

The Sore Spot – locate this by placing your hand over the notch in the base of your throat then moving it down and across slightly, either to the left or right.

Part 2 – The Tapping Sequence

This is the sequence of tapping points you use once you have completed your Set Up. When tapping use your index and middle fingers on your dominant hand. Use sufficient pressure so that you can feel it, but not so much that you hurt yourself.

Using the index and middle fingers, tap 5–7 times on each point as follows using the negative part of your Set-Up Statement (this is also called the 'Reminder Phrase'). Tap on these points:

When you first start tapping it is perfectly normal to experience tingling sensations, pins and needles or even a slight dizziness. This is just your system beginning to relax.

Beginning of the eyebrow

Side of the eye (where you can feel the bone)

Under the eye (where you can feel the bone)

Under the nose

Chin

Collarbone point (where you would knot a tie)

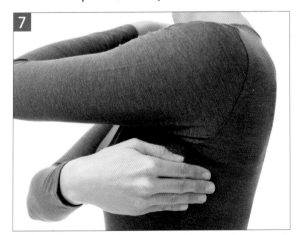

Under the arm (in line with the bra or shirt seam)

Top of the head (using all your fingers in a claw shape)

Please note that although these tapping points proceed down the body, making them easy to memorize, the Sequence finishes at the top of the head. However, it does not seem to matter if you change the order or even forget a point; tapping is a very forgiving process!

At first the simplest way to become proficient with the tapping is to learn this basic Sequence. However, as you become more experienced, you may like to experiment by changing the order in which you tap, or even leaving certain points out. You may find that streamlining the process in this way still works very well for you. However, if you do this and are no longer getting results, all you need to do is revert back to the full Sequence. After all, it only takes a minute or so to do a complete round.

How to progress through the Tapping Sequence

When you apply the tapping, you need to take the negative part from your Set-Up Statement and repeat it aloud while tapping each point in turn. This is called the 'Reminder Phrase' as it keeps you tuned in to the problem. In our example, you have begun your Set Up with: 'Even though I have [this sadness], I deeply and completely love and accept myself.'

So your Reminder Phrase is 'this sadness' and you should repeat this phrase aloud once while you tap on each of the points of the Tapping Sequence. In this way you continually 'remind' your system about the problem you are working on. The best Reminder Phrase is usually identical to the words you choose for the negative part in the Set-Up Statement.

There is really no right or wrong way of doing the tapping. Some people like to tap with their eyes open, others with them closed. Just experiment and find out which feels most natural to you. Equally, there is no specific speed of tapping, you will probably find your rhythm changes with each problem you work on, possibly even each round you do. The only rule here is to do what feels right and appropriate for you.

But let us use another example, this time assuming that you are working on a headache.

There is no right or wrong way of tapping. Just experiment and find out what feels most natural to you.

1. Set Up: Repeat three times while tapping the Karate Chop: 'Even though I have [this dull headache], I deeply and completely love and accept myself.'

2. Tapping Sequence: Repeat the Reminder Phrase 'this dull headache' aloud once while tapping 5–7 times at each of the eight points (see pages 20–21 for photographs):

- Beginning of the eyebrow
- Side of the eye
- Under the eye
- Under the nose
- Chin
- Collarbone point
- Under the arm
- Top of the head

TOP TAPPING TIPS

- You can tap with either hand but you will probably find it more comfortable to use your dominant one.
- Tap with the fingertips of your index finger and middle finger in order to cover the points more easily.
- Tap solidly but never hard enough to hurt.
- Tap 5–7 times on each of the tapping points (although it doesn't matter whether you tap a little more or less).
- Ideally, use all the points, but if you are somewhere where you feel self-conscious, like on the bus, just tap any point you can reach.
- It does not matter which side of the body you tap, the meridians are mirrored on each side. If you feel adventurous you can tap on both sides at the same time (see photos, right and below)!

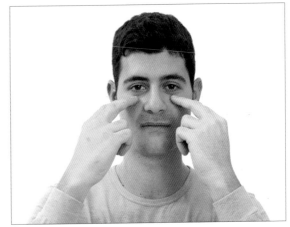

Tapping on both sides: under the eyes...

...under the arms...

...under the nose and on the chin.

Monitoring the changes

Whenever we experience any emotion we also have some form of body sensation – some are obvious, such as butterflies in the tummy, and others are more subtle, such as tightness in the throat. In fact, these sensations tell us we are feeling an emotion – they are the messenger.

Emotions are there for a purpose, they tell us when something is right or wrong for us. Problems arise when we fail to recognize the messages and ignore what our body is telling us. With the tapping you will learn to become more finely tuned to your body's messages and your emotional responses, which in turn will help you manage your emotions in a new way, and ultimately result in a more peaceful inner and outer world.

When you begin this journey of change and self-discovery you are often unable to differentiate between your feelings and the changes in intensity – you just know you feel bad. When you reduce the intensity on an issue and begin to feel a little better, it can be very hard to remember just how strong it was when you started. For this reason, especially when starting to use tapping, it is important to have a way to assess your work. Not only does this validate your results, but it is also very empowering to truly acknowledge your ability to effect positive change on your own. So keep a record for yourself; you will be amazed at what you achieve.

Using the 0–10 scale

In order to keep track of changes we recommend you rate the level of intensity of the emotion, or the physical pain or symptom at the beginning of each round using a scale of 0–10 , where 0 is no intensity at all and 10 is the highest intensity possible. It is a way of measuring the emotional charge of a feeling or memory, or the intensity of a physical pain or symptom. For example, using the headache mentioned in the previous Set Up, you might start the Set Up feeling that your dull headache is somewhere around 9. By the time you finish your first complete round of Tapping Sequence you might feel that your headache had diminished to a rating of 7.

For the next round of tapping you need to change your wording slightly whenever your rating reduces after tapping. The reason for this is that the subconscious mind is very literal and you need to acknowledge the change that has taken place and direct your words and tapping to what remains of the problem.

For example, if you began tapping on a 'dull headache' with an intensity rating of 9, and after a couple of rounds of the Set Up plus the Sequence the intensity has reduced to a 7, you would need to adjust your words while you tap. So for the Set Up you might repeat three times while tapping on the Karate Chop: 'Even though

I still have [some of this dull headache], I deeply and completely love and accept myself.'

You would follow this with the Reminder Phrase in the Tapping Sequence by saying aloud at each point: 'This remaining dull headache'.

And if you assessed how you felt after this, you might assign your headache a rating of 3 and use the phrase in your Set Up: 'Even though I still have [a slightly lingering headache], I deeply and completely love and accept myself.' You

would follow this with the Reminder Phrase in the Tapping Sequence at each point: 'A slightly lingering headache'.

Some people, especially young children, find the numerical scale too difficult, so use whatever works. You could have a scale of colours, which represent different intensities of feelings, or you could assess the intensity spatially, using your arms to illustrate how big the emotional charge feels at any one time. As with everything with the tapping, use the method that works best for you. There really is no right or wrong way here.

Identifying aspects

In order to get complete relief from an issue it is important to understand all the 'aspects', or pieces of the puzzle that make up the problem. If a problem does not clear, it is usually because there is some other aspect interfering with the work. Your job is to become a detective and unearth all these aspects and eliminate them. If tapping doesn't seem to work it is almost always due to undiscovered aspects, not the technique itself.

For example, you may work with your fear of spiders and seem to eliminate it, until a spider scuttles across the room and the fear comes back. In this case, the aspect you have not covered will be a fear of spiders moving and you will need to tap specifically on this. The fear of a stationary spider and the fear of a moving spider are separate problems and need to be addressed separately by tapping.

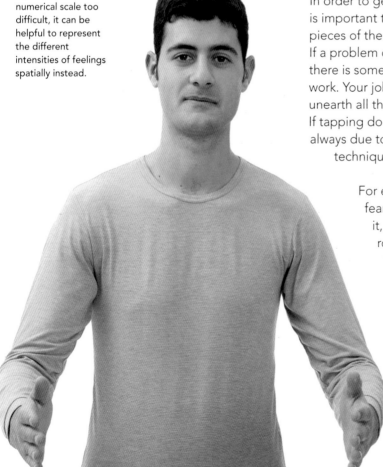

If you find the numerical scale too difficult, it can be helpful to represent the different intensities of feelings spatially instead.

Talking and tapping

Tapping works by talking as you tap on the eight tapping points on your face and body. Throughout this book are tapping 'scripts' for a range of issues – phrases you say while you are tapping on a point. Below are examples of scripts you might use for tapping, with the words shown around the tapping points. While the scripts will give you initial guidance, it is always best to use your own words. When you tap, you are always measuring your response to your words on the tapping scale (see pages 24–25).

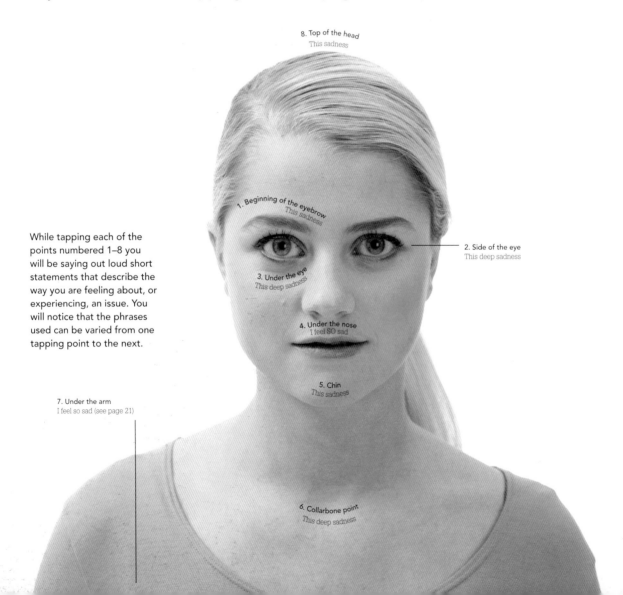

8. Top of the head
This sadness

1. Beginning of the eyebrow
This sadness

2. Side of the eye
This deep sadness

3. Under the eye
This deep sadness

4. Under the nose
I feel SO sad

5. Chin
This sadness

6. Collarbone point
This deep sadness

7. Under the arm
I feel so sad (see page 21)

While tapping each of the points numbered 1–8 you will be saying out loud short statements that describe the way you are feeling about, or experiencing, an issue. You will notice that the phrases used can be varied from one tapping point to the next.

8. Top of the head
This headache

1. Beginning of the eyebrow
This headache

2. Side of the eye
This dull headache

3. Under the eye
This dull headache

4. Under the nose
My head aches SO much

5. Chin
This headache

7. Under the arm
My head aches SO much
(see page 21)

6. Collarbone point
This dull headache

The phrases you choose to describe what you are experiencing need to be short enough for you to say them out loud as you are tapping on each of the points roughly 5–7 times.

Tapping in pairs

Tapping with another person is a useful alternative to tapping on your own. It can be an additional support to have someone guide you through the process. There are two ways to tap in pairs.

Mirror tapping

The first way is to sit opposite one another, mirroring the tapping points. Take a moment or two to tune in to each other and match your breathing and posture. This creates rapport. As the guide, your role is to listen and to help the other person formulate a Set-Up Statement that describes the problem, and then lead the tapping by saying the phrases you have agreed out loud first.

As the guide, you speak on behalf of the other person, as if you were them. So for instance, if they are addressing a feeling of anger, your Set-Up Statement might be: 'Even though I have [this anger], I deeply and completely love and accept myself'. As the guide you say this first, then it is repeated by your partner, who is the one experiencing the feeling of anger.

Mirror tapping, which involves sitting opposite your partner and mirroring the tapping points, is a useful alternative to tapping on your own.

Tapping on a partner

Tapping on another person can be a very powerful experience for both people involved. However, in the role of guide you should always ask the other person's permission first.

Next make sure you are sitting in a position to comfortably reach and tap on the other person. Take a moment to tune in to each other by matching breathing and posture.

Then your role as guide is to listen, help your partner to formulate a statement that describes the problem, and then lead the process by tapping each of the points in turn, saying the phrases you have agreed out loud. You need to apply enough pressure to each point for the other person to feel it, but not enough to cause them to flinch or tense up.

Many people enjoy the experience of being tapped on and find that it frees them to tune in exclusively to their internal process. The deep connection and intimacy that it creates is healing in its own right.

In the same way as when you are mirror tapping in pairs (see opposite), when tapping on another person as the guide you speak on behalf of the other person, as if you were them. So for instance, if they are addressing a nervous feeling of butterflies in their tummy, your Set-Up Statement might be: 'Even though I have [these butterflies in my tummy], I deeply and completely love and accept myself.'

As the guide, you say this first, then it is repeated by your partner, who is the one experiencing the nervous feeling.

Tapping on a partner promotes a deep sense of intimacy and connection, which is healing in its own right.

Chapter 2

CLASSIC EFT TECHNIQUES

'Mastering classic EFT techniques will dramatically enhance your emotional and physical health and well-being.'

The Movie Technique will help you to take charge of the way you view your world.

Your tapping toolbox

While you can get started with EFT by simply learning the tapping points, there are a number of techniques and refinements that can dramatically enhance your self-work, helping you to gain results even more easily and smoothly. None of these techniques are complex and all are worthy of attention in their own right.

Take time to read through the techniques outlined in this chapter, as they will help lead you to a deeper understanding of the power of tapping and how you can apply it to yourself. They are the foundational processes as taught by the EFT founder, Gary Craig, and are an essential part of any tapping toolbox. Once you are familiar with using them you will be able to dramatically enhance your general emotional and physical health and well-being. Mastering the techniques detailed below will form the basis of all your self-work.

The Movie Technique

The mainstay of all your work with EFT, the Movie Technique is a gentle way to resolve traumatic memories without revisiting them in depth.

Throughout the book you will be asked to use this technique. You simply choose a memory of something that is finished in real time but which still disturbs you in some way when you bring it to mind. In your mind, make this memory into a mini movie with you in it, and imagine that you can watch it on the wall opposite.

HOW LONG DOES IT RUN?

To allow this technique to work easily you want a movie that is no more than five minutes long, preferably less. It may be that a specific movie contains many different pieces. If so, you will need to treat each piece or segment of the movie separately with the tapping.

Exercise

1. Bring to mind a memory of a troubling event from your past. Imagine that you have a camera in your mind and zoom into the segment of each memory that carries the main emotional charge. It may be a look on someone's face, something somebody said, or the moment an accident happened. You want to find THAT moment, the moment out of the whole memory that contains the highest intensity of emotion.

2. Give that segment a short title that specifically represents the movie for you. The only reason for making it relatively short is that you will be tapping around all the points using it as the Reminder Phrase. For example: 'Three years old, Dad hitting me in the kitchen' is more precise and specific than 'Dad hitting me'. If your dad hit you once, the chances are he hit you several times and there may be a number of memories that could fit under that general title. You will need to treat each one as a separate incident.

3. Quickly rate your movie on a scale of 0–10 on how you feel about it NOW, not then but NOW. If you don't know, guess. If you don't feel anything about it but think you should, just guess at how much you think you SHOULD feel about it and treat it in the same way.

4. Now start tapping as follows, simply following the movie title with either 'movie' or 'emotion'. When you have tapped on it for maybe four or five rounds, if no emotional response reveals itself then you are clear on that particular memory; it is not contributing to the way you live your life now. However, if you are repressing or avoiding the emotions underneath it, and you start to get a sense of these, continue tapping, following your emotional or physical responses.

5. So start by repeating three times while tapping the Karate Chop: 'Even though I have [this X movie] I deeply and completely love and accept myself.' (You fill in the X with whatever emotion or phrase that is relevant to you.)

6. Follow this by tapping the Tapping Sequence using the Reminder Phrase 'this X movie' on each of the eight points (see pages 20–21). While saying the phrase aloud tap 5–7 times on the beginning of the eyebrow, side of the eye, under the eye, under the nose, chin, collarbone point, under the arm and finally the top of the head.

7. Again, repeat three times while tapping the Karate Chop the Set-Up Statement: 'Even though I have [these X movie emotions] I deeply and completely love and accept myself.'

8. Follow this by tapping the Tapping Sequence using the Reminder Phrase 'these X movie emotions' on each of the eight points (see pages 20–21). While saying the phrase aloud tap 5–7 times on the beginning of the eyebrow, side of the eye, under the eye, under the nose, chin, collarbone point, under the arm and finally the top of the head.

You might choose an alternative phrase for the Set-Up Statement: 'Even though I have [these X emotions], I deeply and completely love and accept myself', followed by the Reminder Phrase in the Tapping Sequence 'these X emotions'.

9. Continue tapping both the Set-Up Statement and the Reminder Phrases until you feel comfortable enough to watch the movie. Check your 0–10 rating and note your intensity score now when you think about the movie. Continue tapping as above until you feel a significant reduction in the intensity. In your mind's eye, run the movie on the wall opposite you, noticing any segment that still has an emotional charge.

10. Stop at the segment and repeat three times while tapping the Karate Chop: 'Even though I [feel 'X' at that bit], I deeply and completely love and accept myself.' Follow this by the Reminder Phrases in the Tapping Sequence. At this point you may use variations on the Reminder Phrase as indicated below:

Beginning of the eyebrow ... *Feeling X at that bit*
Side of the eye .... *That bit*
Under the eye................................. *Still getting me*
Under the nose.....................*Still making me feel X*
Chin..*Feeling X at that bit*
Collarbone point .... *That bit*

Under the arm .... *Still getting me*
Top of the head ....*Still making me feel X*

11. Once you have reduced the intensity on 'that bit' you may want to change your language to describe what 'that bit' is. It may be the words that someone used. For example, continue by tapping the Karate Chop three times and repeating: 'Even though [he said that], I deeply and completely love and accept myself'. Follow this with the Tapping Sequence using the Reminder Phrase 'He said that', and variations of the phrase, as indicated below:

Beginning of the eyebrow ....*He said that*
Side of the eye .... *Those words*
Under the eye..*His words*
Under the nose.................................. *He said that*
Chin............................... *I can't believe he said that*
Collarbone point .... *Those words*
Under the arm ....*He said that*
Top of the head ....*His words*

Continue the process until you can run the entire movie in one go without getting any charge. At this point it may seem like you are watching someone else in that situation, it might turn into black and white, or it may have moved very far away. Sometimes you may not be able to see it at all anymore. It will not make what happened OK, but it will prevent you from feeling the pain of it in your life today.

12. When you feel that you can run the movie from start to finish without any emotional charge, move on to the next technique, the Telling the Story Technique.

The Telling the Story Technique

This technique is another way of coming to terms with your emotions and negative memories and follows on directly from the Movie Technique.

Exercise

1. Start by imagining telling someone the story of one of your negative memories. How do you feel when you think about telling that story? Rate the intensity of your feelings on the 0–10 scale. Is it OK to share the story or do you feel anxious, embarrassed, frightened or some other uncomfortable emotion?

2. If the idea of telling the story makes you feel uncomfortable, complete the following Sequence before starting to tell the story. Start by repeating three times while tapping the Karate Chop: 'Even though I have this [telling the story anxiety/embarrassment/fear], I deeply and completely love and accept myself.' Follow this by tapping the Tapping Sequence using the Reminder Phrase 'telling the story anxiety' on each of the eight points (see pages 20–21). While saying the phrase aloud tap 5–7 times on the beginning of the eyebrow, side of the eye, under the eye, under the nose, chin, collarbone point, under the arm and finally the top of the head.

3. When you have cleared your initial feelings about telling the story you can start to imagine telling it. As with the Movie Technique, when you reach a point in the story that feels uncomfortable, for whatever reason, stop and tap on that bit. For example: Repeat three times while tapping the Karate Chop: 'Even though I feel [too embarrassed to talk about that bit], I deeply and completely love and accept myself.' Follow this by tapping the Tapping Sequence using

By using the Telling the Story Technique, you will come to realize that 'you are not your story'.

variations of the Reminder Phrase: 'Embarrassed at that bit' and 'This embarrassment' on each of the eight points (as above).

4. Again, repeat the following statement three times while tapping the Karate Chop: 'Even though I feel [ashamed when I think of that bit], I deeply and completely love and accept myself.' Follow this by tapping the Tapping Sequence using variations of the Reminder Phrase: 'This shame' and 'Shame at that bit' on each of the eight points (as above).

5. Remember to keep checking in on your 0–10 scale. Continue until you can 'tell the story' without any emotional charge.

If you can actually test this by really talking it through with somebody, for instance a therapist or a good friend, somebody you can trust, then go ahead and do it. However, it is important to take care of yourself at all times, and it may not be appropriate for other people to know these stories; they are private for whatever reason and that is fine, so respect your own privacy here. No one else needs to know; all that matters is that you are able to clear any ongoing negative emotional response to your story.

The Chasing the Pain Technique

It is very common for pains to change and relocate around the body when we tap. Your perception may be, for instance, that you have had the same chronic back pain for five years, only to find that the pain actually shifts from the lower left side to upper right after a round or two of tapping.

You might also find that the quality of the pain changes from sharp to dull. We don't know for sure how this happens, but one possible explanation is that pain itself is created by stuck energy that begins to clear once the tapping is applied. Given that the nature of energy is one of movement and flow, once a block is released the energy flows freely until it meets another obstruction, again tappable. Imagine yourself as an energetic plumber, gently releasing any

blocks to the free flowing of the body's energy. Since observing this phenomenon of pain moving around the body as a consequence of tapping, we have called the technique used to deal with this pain relocation the Chasing the Pain Technique. It involves 'chasing' the physical sensations or symptoms around your body and tapping at each location. It is fascinating to discover for yourself that seemingly intractable problems with a genuine physical cause can change and even clear as you tap.

To allow the Chasing the Pain Technique to work effectively, it is very important to follow three basic rules – concerning location, quality and intensity.

Mastering the Chasing the Pain Technique will help you to learn the language of your body.

RULE 1: LOCATION

Describe to yourself the exact location of the pain. Be specific. In the same way a postcode will direct you to a precise address, you need to instruct your subconscious mind to the exact location of the discomfort. For example, 'the tip of my left shoulder blade', or 'the top of my right thigh' are more precise than 'my shoulder blade' or 'my right thigh'.

RULE 2: QUALITY

Pain has many different qualities – it can be sharp, dull, hot, constant or throbbing. The word 'pain' itself may not be right; you may experience it as an ache, a stiffness or a hurt. Make sure your wording accurately reflects the symptom.

RULE 3: INTENSITY

Once you have isolated the location of the pain and named the quality of the pain, use the 0–10 scale to rate the intensity of the pain right now.

Using these three rules will also give you three different measures of change to monitor before and after tapping on pain. The idea that pain can move or change quality – as well as go up or down in intensity in response to tapping often gives us a healthy expectancy about what else might be possible.

Here is an example of the kind of phrases that would be typical of Chasing the Pain Technique. Adjust the actual words, following the same principles, to suit your own situation.

Exercise

1. Start by repeating three times while tapping the Karate Chop: 'Even though I have [this sharp pain on the right side of my neck], I deeply and completely love and accept myself.' Follow this by tapping the Tapping Sequence using the Reminder Phrase 'this sharp pain on the right side of my neck' on each of the eight points (see pages 20–21). While saying the phrase aloud, tap 5–7 times on the beginning of the eyebrow, side of the eye, under the eye, under the nose, chin, collarbone point, under the arm and finally the top of the head.

2. Then tune back into your symptom and see what has happened to the pain. Check the location, quality and intensity. If any of these has changed, alter your words accordingly. For instance, perhaps the above 'sharp pain on the right side of my neck' feels roughly the same on the 0–10 intensity scale, but has moved to the left side and is no longer sharp but feels like it is spreading out. Also the word 'pain' is no longer exactly right – it actually feels more like an ache. Now you need to change your words as follows.

3. Continue by repeating three times while tapping the Karate Chop: 'Even though I have [this spreading ache on the left side of my neck], I deeply and completely love and accept myself.' Follow this by tapping the Tapping Sequence using the Reminder Phrase 'this spreading ache on the left side of my neck' on each of the eight points (see pages 20–21).

4. Keep monitoring your pain and adjust the words in both your Set-Up Statement and Reminder Phrase until the pain is clear or at least substantially reduced in intensity.

The Constricted Breathing Technique

We are all familiar to some extent with the body–mind connection. We know the toll that stress can take on our bodies. Perhaps you are also aware of the way that anxiety often shows up in our breathing.

The Constricted Breathing Technique is a nifty way of reducing generalized anxiety without having to go deeper into your issues, or even to work out what you are anxious about at a specific point in time.

We all experience certain levels of anxiety in our everyday lives – these anxieties may be classified as low-level and normal, but they can accumulate and our overall stress levels rise accordingly, often without our noticing until we develop more pressing symptoms such as migraines or high blood pressure.

If you build the Constricted Breathing Technique into your daily health routine, perhaps doing it in the morning and evening when you clean your teeth (it will only take you a couple of minutes), you will be surprised at how much better you feel generally after a week or so. You probably spend more time than this in the bath or on the computer, so why not add this technique to your daily routine and reap the benefits of a calmer, healthier life?

Exercise

1. Take a couple of deep breaths to stretch out your lungs. Next, take the fullest breath possible for you right now and rate it on a scale of 0–10, where 0 is no breath at all and 10 is the fullest breath that you can imagine taking. With that information you can move on to the Tapping Sequence.

2. Start by repeating three times while tapping the Karate Chop: 'Even though I have this [constricted breathing], I deeply and completely love and accept myself.' Continue by repeating three times while tapping the Karate Chop: 'Even though [something is blocking my fullest breath], I deeply and completely love and accept myself.'

3. Follow this by tapping the Tapping Sequence using the Reminder Phrases 'this constricted breathing' and 'something is blocking my breathing' or variations on these. While saying the phrase aloud tap 5–7 times on the beginning of the eyebrow, side of the eye, under the eye, under the nose, chin, collarbone point, under the arm and finally the top of the head.

4. Continue tapping on each of the eight points (see pages 20–21) using the following Reminder Phrases or variations of these: 'This remaining constricted breathing', 'This remaining block to my fullest breath' and 'This remaining something blocking my breath'.

5. Reassess your breath. Chances are your breathing will be deeper or more expansive, or have changed quality in some way. Sometimes a snippet of a memory or an emotion may surface. If this is the case, make a note in your journal to work with it, as it will be important and relevant in some way, even if that is not clear now.

With the Constricted Breathing Technique, you can tap to expand your breathing and enjoy increased health and vitality.

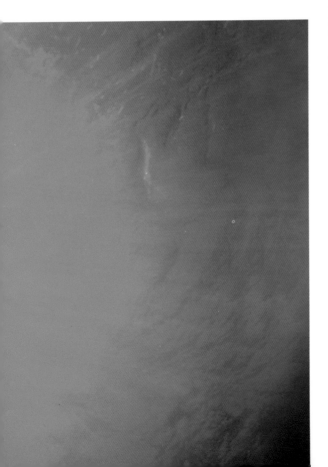

TOP TAPPING TIPS – CLASSIC EFT TECHNIQUES

BE SPECIFIC
These are the buzzwords of EFT. The more specific you are when naming the problem, the quicker the results. You are always looking for the specific piece of the puzzle that holds the problem state in place; it may be a look, a voice tone, a specific thought, memory or emotion.

TEST YOUR WORK CONTINUALLY THROUGHOUT THE SESSION, NOT JUST AT THE END
This is vital. Continually test as you work, always looking to find any hidden unresolved aspects. Use the 0–10 scale.

TAP REGULARLY
Make tapping part of your daily routine...how long does it take? Notice any resistance to doing this. Tap on it using these Set-Up Statements.
- 'Even though I don't want to tap I deeply and completely love and accept myself.'
- 'Even though I don't have the time to tap I deeply and completely love and accept myself.'
- 'Even though I am too tired to tap I deeply and completely love and accept myself.'

Chapter 3

EFT INNOVATIONS

'As tapping becomes more widespread and gains in popularity, new techniques are being developed to enhance and expand the practice. Here we present the most effective and user-friendly of these innovations.'

Reconnect to the wisdom of your heart by working with the Heart Anchor.

EFT innovations

As EFT has become more widespread and gained in popularity, a number of highly experienced practitioners have developed techniques to enhance and expand our work even further. We have selected a few techniques that we have found to be particularly effective and user-friendly, including how to begin to work with positive states.

In Chapter 4 we will introduce you to the Personal Peace Procedure, a technique that was developed by EFT founder Gary Craig. While this technique is certainly an innovative way of working, and perhaps deserves to appear in this chapter too, it is such an important part of our self-work with the tapping that we have given it a chapter in its own right. You will come to learn that we use it for a very specific purpose, namely to heal our past history.

The Heart Anchor

Developed by Sue Beer, the Heart Anchor is a way of working with the energy of the heart. This technique uses two extra points and is a simple way to develop your connection to your own wisdom and strength. You can begin using it right away, however insurmountable your problems may seem.

Whenever we have a problem, we are inevitably very focused on the negative thoughts and feelings that are attached to it. And this, of course, is where we begin with EFT. The Heart Anchor, however, is a unique EFT innovation that takes advantage of a potential often completely overlooked when we are in the problem state. Just as a plant will always grow towards the light, there is an innate human tendency towards healing. (For more information you might be interested in Sue's book *Healing the Addicted Heart: the Five Stages of Transformation*.)

The Heart Anchor harnesses this idea and builds on it by working with the energetic vibration of the heart, our emotional centre and the seat of our true wisdom. It is very easy to do, and is not only extremely powerful, but gives us a gift which is with us wherever we are, and at any time we need to bring ourselves back to centre and peacefulness. It is a practical way of activating the positive potential within each one of us (which has always been there, but gets hidden beneath the traumas and stresses of our life experiences). Using it regularly begins to change our experience of the way we live our lives.

The realization, even in the midst of some kind of problem, that it is still possible to access and cultivate positive feelings is a powerful one. Indeed it is the beginning of self-empowerment. You can use the Heart Anchor on its own, as well as alongside the EFT tapping points. You will quickly begin to notice that developing your Heart Anchor supercharges your work with EFT. Most of the case studies that follow show the power of using the Heart Anchor alongside tapping. Look for the Heart Anchor symbol throughout the text (see box, below).

HEART ANCHOR SYMBOL

This symbol represents the Heart Anchor. In a nutshell, the Heart Anchor reconnects us to Love with a capital L. It triggers an inherently internal state of Love that is there in each and every one of us regardless of our current problems. To build a strong Heart Anchor, begin by holding the two points described on pages 44–5 while thinking about/seeing/looking at something that gives you pleasure: maybe a favourite person or pet, a piece of music or a blue sky. Over time, keep adding more pleasurable experiences to the Heart Anchor while holding these points.

ACTIVATING YOUR HEART ANCHOR

The Heart Anchor is very practical. You begin simply by touching the specific Heart Anchor points (see below) and noticing how this feels. You may feel tingling or warmth, or you may not feel anything at all to begin with. Your job is simply to notice, without judgement. Then the next step is to touch the points again, and at the same time bring to mind anything that unfailingly makes you feel good or brings a smile to your face. Perhaps this is your favourite pet or person; or maybe it is a wonderful scene, colour or memory. This begins to create a positive association (or anchor) to the energy points that you are touching. This is the beginning of training the brain's capacity for happiness and good feelings.

HEART ANCHOR POINTS

There are two points in the Heart Anchor. Initially, it is important to find them and try them out without any particular expectation. To do this, first put one hand on the centre of your chest (or heart chakra area) and gently rub. This is the heart point and it is connected to an invisible network of energy channels that spread out and open up the lungs and chest area.

Then place your other hand at the back of your head at the base of the skull, where you would cradle a baby's head, and rub both points lightly at the same time. There is literally and energetically a pathway here that runs from the heart to the emotional brain.

Sense that pathway and then sense it going beyond the constraints of your physical body. You may or may not notice tingling, energy moving or some other shift in your physiology as you touch these points. Either way is fine.

DEVELOPING THE HEART ANCHOR

Once you have 'tested' the Heart Anchor points you are ready to continue to the next stage.

Exercise

1. Close your eyes and go into the Heart Anchor pose with one hand on your heart and the other at the base of your skull (see above). Rub both points lightly at the same time.

2. With your eyes still closed, focus on the physical sensations coming from the centre – your heart – radiating out into those tiny fine channels…opening the heart area and connecting the heart to the mind. And, if you like, zoom into the very heart centre, and as you do, maybe you can remember a time you felt really loving…or you were surprisingly successful at something. Maybe some pleasant memory presents itself to you now…a smile, your favourite person, pet or special place…

3. Now open your eyes and come out of the pose. Take a deep breath in and out.

4. Close your eyes again and go back in with your hands on both Heart Anchor points – notice how quickly those feelings come back. Let any pictures fade now so that you are focusing entirely on the feeling response as you lightly rub the two points. Ask yourself:

- How does it feel?
- Where is the feeling?
- How does it move?
- What is the texture of the feeling?
- Does it make a sound?
- What colour is it?
- What temperature?
- Where is the warmest part?

5. Open your eyes and come out again. Take another deep breath in and out. Go back in for a few seconds.

6. From now on, whenever you feel good for any reason, maybe simply seeing a lovely flower or the sun breaking through the clouds, notice your good feelings and touch your Heart Anchor points just for a moment. Very soon, you will notice a flood of good feelings when you touch the Heart Anchor points, whatever the actual circumstances you are in.

Once you have spent a bit of time strengthening your Heart Anchor, you can add it to your EFT work, as well as generally having it available as you go about your everyday life.

It is especially useful when working with some of the techniques mentioned in the previous chapter (see pages 30–39). Once you have reduced the charge on a negative memory, thought or belief to a manageable number, perhaps below 5, fire your Heart Anchor and notice how it feels to be thinking the same thing or viewing the same memory from this new place. You will be amazed at how different things look from this vantage point!

Gently rub the first Heart Anchor point, in the centre of the chest.

At the same time, rub the second point at the back of your head.

The two Heart Anchor points are located in the centre of the chest and at the base of the skull at the back of the head.

Imaginary Tapping

The subconscious mind does not know the difference between fact and fiction. When you vividly imagine something you really do experience it. You may already have experienced this phenomenon in the way that past traumas can feel very real in the present.

Most of us have had the experience of reliving memories, both positive and negative, and of them seeming as real in the moment as they were at the time they happened.

For those of you who haven't, vividly imagine holding half a lemon and then squeeze some of the juice into your mouth. Are you salivating?

Vividly imagine tapping when your location or circumstances make it difficult to physically tap.

Do you have a lemon? Imaginary Tapping can be very effective at times when you can't physically tap, such as during an MRI scan. It is also useful at night when the physical body is too tired to tap.

In those times when your body is exhausted but your mind is active, doing the actual tapping can serve to wake the body up too – not for everyone, but it is worth trying the Imaginary Tapping as a viable alternative.

It is useful to practise Imaginary Tapping before you actually need it so that you are able to just draw on this skill in the moment. When setting up the Imaginary Tapping you want to create a full sensory experience, imagine how it feels, dwelling on each point until you are really able to recreate the sensation of your fingers touching your skin. Then imagine what you might hear. If you listen very carefully you will become aware of the sound of your fingers tapping on you. Then notice what you are saying to yourself, in the privacy of your mind, as you tap around the points. Really take your time to train your mind to build the experience up so that it becomes truly alive for you. Remember our lemon!

Here's how you do it.

Exercise

1. Identify something to tap on.

2. Close your eyes.

3. Imagine or visualize tapping around the Tapping Sequence points (see pages 20–21): Beginning of the eyebrow, Side of the eye, Under the eye, Under the nose, Chin, Collarbone point, Under the arm, and finally, at the Top of head.

Tap and Rant!

Forget politeness and social niceties; tell it as it is! In other words, speak the truth about how you feel, warts and all. Swear, curse, do whatever it takes to honestly put the emotions on the table for healing.

It is amazing how many of us censor ourselves by trying to 'be polite', 'be nice' and 'say the right thing'. We make all sorts of self-judgements about how we feel and how we should feel. But who dictates how we should feel? And whose rules are we following when we try to disguise our truth? When we censor ourselves we devalue both ourselves and our emotions. After all, the sole purpose of emotions is to give us an indictation of whether something is or is not OK for us – for example, whether you should relax or be on guard in a particular situation.

Most of us will find that we are not honouring our true feelings for reasons which, when brought under the spotlight, are often outdated. But while these feelings – and the beliefs that underpin them – go unattended, the internal conflict tends to manifest itself physically, whether in the form of stress, disease, exhaustion or some other ailment.

Maybe you feel that if you express your emotions honestly you may harm a loved one. And this may be true – if you tell them outright, that is. However, while you keep quiet on the account of other people, the feelings you are hiding may be harming you. If this is how you feel, try tapping and ranting.

Dedicate some time and space to yourself and release all the stuff that is churning in your mind – out loud preferably – while tapping. Those negative thoughts, and the inner dialogue that accompanies them, are disrupting your energy system, so rather than trying to stop it, let it out and tap at the same time to clear it. This technique is highly effective. And it can be fun to let rip, too!

Exercise

1. Start by identifying something that you would like to tap on.

2. Repeat three times while tapping the Karate Chop: 'Even though [it wasn't fair] I deeply and completely love and accept myself.'

3. Tap the Tapping Sequence using Reminder Phrases on each of the eight points (see pages 20–21). As you tap each of the points, vary your Reminder Phrases. For example:

Beginning of the eyebrow .... *It wasn't fair*
Side of the eye .... *It shouldn't have happened*
Under the eye .... *I'm really angry with X*
Under the nose .... *I am really hurt*
Chin .... *This sadness*
Collarbone point .... *He/she is a...*
Under the arm .... *I hate him/her*
Top of the head .... *How could he/she do that?*

We cannot change other people or their behaviours, but we can change our response to them. We have a choice, and this particular method of tapping helps us to activate that choice by releasing the hurts, judgements and negative beliefs that we carry around in our lives – these are not our truths, they are merely the illusions that we run on. By Tapping and Ranting, we can change this and take charge of our lives in a positive way.

Continual Tapping

Developed by our Australian friend and colleague, Dr David Lake, this technique is especially useful at times when it is not possible to tap the full Sequence. It is also good as a general habit to get into (without having to address any problem), when watching TV or going out for a walk. It allows us to release everyday niggles and anxieties that we take for granted, without the need to isolate them or find out what they are specifically.

In the 21st century most of us experience varying degrees of stress in our everyday lives. And often we are not even aware of it; we normalize our experience and become acclimatized to living in this way. Stress accumulates, ultimately taking its toll on our physical well-being in the long term. By getting into the habit of Continual Tapping we are able to release these stresses easily without even having to think about them. Try it for yourself – after a month of using the Continual Tapping whenever you have the opportunity (basically when you are not needing your hands for anything else) you will be amazed at how different you feel and how your general energy and well-being have improved.

David and his colleague Steve Wells refer to it as energy toning. Continually tapping the finger points as described below stimulates the majority of the energy meridians and, while arguably not as powerful as the full Tapping Sequence, has been shown to give very impressive results.

FINGER TAPPING

One key advantage of this method of tapping is that it can be done anywhere and is unobtrusive. Performers and public speakers will often hold a hand behind their back or in a pocket and tap while working in order to stabilize their energy and calm excessive nervousness. It is a neat trick to have up your sleeve before any potentially difficult time, maybe a tricky meeting with the boss or having to speak publicly. Once you know how easy it is then you can keep a hand under the desk or the like and tap while you are in the meeting itself – you will be surprised how effective it is!

Keep a look out for people using this discreet version of tapping – you may be amazed where you spot it. Reports so far include celebrities, sports personalities and captains of industry, to name but a few!

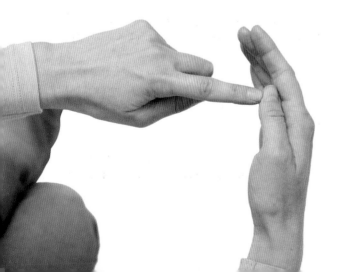

Continual Tapping is a handy technique that you can use to rebalance yourself as you go about your daily life.

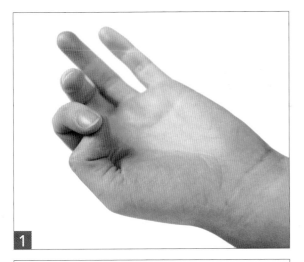

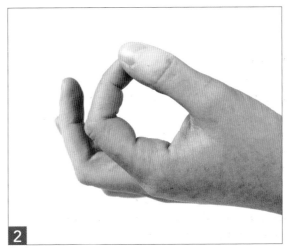

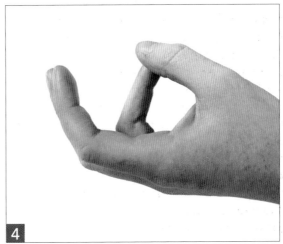

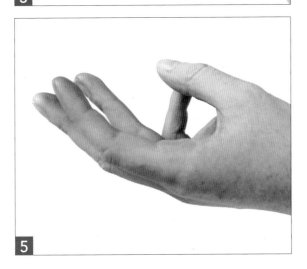

Exercise

1. Using your index finger, tap on the inside of the thumb along the nail bed facing the body (see opposite, 1).

2. Then use the thumb to tap the same position on each of the four fingers (see opposite, 2, 3, 4 and 5).

3. Get a rhythm going and tap continuously. There is no need to tune into anything specific.

Chapter 4

HEAL THE PAST

'It is possible to work through all our traumatic memories and clear our limiting beliefs, which in turn allows us to move through our blocks in the here and now until we are able to fully engage with life joyously.'

Processing difficult memories

With EFT we have discovered a highly effective method of healing the past, and the good news is that we can do most of it for ourselves. Through the journey of life bad things happen. That is the case for all of us, whether it is a major trauma such as a car crash, rape or divorce, or the more minor mini traumas of everyday life, such as being told off by a teacher, having a fight in the playground, being cut up when driving, or having a run-in with the boss.

There is no difference in the way these traumatic memories are stored in our minds. However, some memories continue to elicit an emotional response, whereas others, even more traumatic ones, may feel truly over and have taken their place in your personal history. This becomes a problem in the present day when events that remain unprocessed by our subconscious minds still show up in the way we live our daily lives.

For example, the child who was told off in class for making a mistake in a maths test may well be living their adult life believing that they are bad at maths. It is these events, and the faulty childhood decisions we make about ourselves and the world, which conspire to restrict and block us in our lives today. We take on beliefs about ourselves that are merely illusions, yet we treat them as truths and behave accordingly.

This is where tapping becomes really exciting. It is possible to work through all our traumatic memories (no matter how minor they may seem) and clear our limiting beliefs, which in turn allows us to move through our blocks in the here and now until we are able to fully engage with life joyously. We are not wiping our memory banks (that would not be useful in any case), we are merely clearing our emotional responses to what happened to us and updating our internal technology and map of the world. Sounds too good to be true? So how do we do this?

HEART ANCHOR
(See pages 43–45 for more information)

How might you use your Heart Anchor to heal the past?
After tapping to clear the negative feelings associated with a memory, hold the Heart Anchor points and send love to all the people involved. What happens when you send love to the people who hurt you? Or to people you may have hurt?

ASK QUESTIONS AND FACE THE ISSUES

• When was the first time I felt this?

_____

_____

_____

• What was happening?

_____

_____

_____

• What happens in my body when I remember that now?

_____

_____

_____

• How long does that specific memory take to play itself out in my mind?

_____

_____

_____

• What is the worst bit of the memory, the bit that carries the highest charge?

_____

_____

_____

The Personal Peace Procedure

One of the fundamental tapping processes is the Personal Peace Procedure, developed by EFT founder Gary Craig. Gary says that 'properly understood, this technique should be the healing centrepiece for every person on earth. Diligently using this process will propel each individual towards personal peace, which, in turn, contributes mightily towards world peace'. We very much echo those words.

When it is effectively applied, the Personal Peace Procedure revolutionizes our present by releasing the emotional baggage we all carry with us. It is a way of working through your residual emotional attachments to past events, and to all those memories that, when you bring them to mind now, still have a charge on them, still make you feel cross, embarrassed, shameful, or sad. And you can do it for yourself.

Some memories, when you bring them to mind now, feel genuinely over and done with. You know something happened, but you don't feel disturbed when you remember it now. It really is over. And it isn't disturbing your energy system.

However, other memories, maybe your first romance or something like that, may still have a charge when you bring them to mind now. For example, you may feel embarrassed or hot or shaky or scared. Those memories that 'get' you in some way now, yet are over in real time, are those that are still creating a disruption in your energy system today.

These are the memories that you need to work through and clear using the Personal Peace Procedure. This accumulation of unresolved history contributes to the more global manifestations of dis-ease – depression, panic attacks, general malaise and serious disease.

You may be asking whether it's normal to have an emotional response to something bad. Well, yes of course it is normal. Working like this is not going to make you an emotionless zombie, but it will allow you greater emotional freedom. Your subconscious mind will only clear whatever it deems to be 'excess emotion' for you.

For example, if someone dies it is normal to be sad, but if they died 20 years ago and you are still crying about them every day and it is preventing you from enjoying your life fully, then that is possibly an excessive emotional response. Those are the responses we are looking to change here, those that 'get' you in some way in the here and now, but are over in real time and belong on the shelf with the other history books.

Systematically working through your own Personal Peace Procedure, as described in the following text, will allow you to feel better generally, move through your limiting beliefs and blocks, and be less susceptible to ongoing stressors in your life today.

Beginning your journey

So, the first thing to do is buy yourself a beautiful notebook to begin your new journey. Divide it into sections, each one representing a decade of your life. Under each decade bring to mind any memory that still carries a charge on it today – if you are not sure, write it down anyway. List both obvious big 'T' traumas and the little 't' traumas, the everyday traumas, they are all valuable to work through. If there are some things that happened which you can't remember but others tell you about and you feel you SHOULD have a response to, put these down on the list anyway.

You may want to divide each decade into relevant sections such as:

• School
• Home
• Siblings
• Parents
• Family
• Husband/wife/partner
• Children
• Romantic relationships
• Work
• Friends
• Other

Most people typically make a list of 50–100 of these memories straight off. Don't worry if you seem to have a lot more or if you seem to have fewer, just do your best to write down what happened: 'the betrayal', 'the accident', 'he left me', and that kind of thing. And by each memory note an intensity rating for how strongly you feel about that now, not how strongly you think you might have felt back then. Once you have your list, the idea is that you take one, or at an absolute maximum two, of these memories a day and work through them using the tapping.

Make each memory into a mini movie, imagining that you can watch it on the wall opposite, with you in the movie (see pages 33–34 for more about the Movie Technique).

You need to name your movie, since you will be using the title when tapping. For example, suppose you have a memory from school of being called up in front of the whole class and of feeling humiliated; a good title to give that movie might include the name of the teacher, say 'Mrs Brown humiliated me'. In this way you are able to identify a particular time and place, and also the feelings and emotions that went with the memory. Then, to make this work really effectively, imagine that you have the camera in your mind and you can zoom in to the bit of the memory that still has the main emotional crescendo for you today. It could be the look on Mrs Brown's face, or the sound or tone of her voice, or it could be the way that she swung round to the blackboard. Whatever it is, zoom in on it and edit your movie down so that it would be somewhere between 30 seconds to two minutes long maximum if you were really watching it.

Assess the intensity of feeling as you bring that movie to mind now, using our scale of 0–10 (for more about the scale see pages 24–25).

Exercise: Heal the past

So let us go through a complete first round of working on a memory to heal your past. Remember, you need to select a traumatic memory from your personal history, then make that memory into a mini movie, imagining that you can watch it on the wall opposite, with you in the movie.

1 Start by repeating three times while tapping the Karate Chop: 'Even though I have this [Mrs Brown humiliated me movie], I deeply and completely love and accept myself.'

2 Follow this by tapping the Tapping Sequence using the Reminder Phrase 'Mrs Brown humiliated me movie' or variations, 'She humiliated me' or 'Mrs Brown humiliated me emotions' on each of the eight points (see pages 20–21). While saying the phrase aloud, tap 5–7 times on each point.

Mrs Brown humiliated me movie

Mrs Brown humiliated me movie

She humiliated me

She really humiliated me

Mrs Brown humiliated me movie

Mrs Brown humiliated me movie

Mrs Brown humiliated me emotions

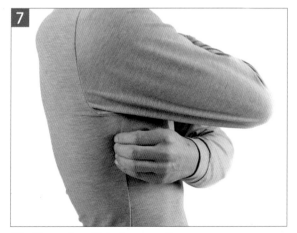

Mrs Brown humiliated me emotions

3 When you have done one or two rounds, rate the intensity of your emotions again on the 0–10 scale. Perhaps you began at 8, so once the intensity has fallen to somewhere between 4 and 6, for instance, notice what is actually happening in your body. Has some kind of physical sensation emerged such as heaviness in your stomach or tightness in your throat? Has some other emotion such as sadness or anger emerged? In which case you would then make a Set-Up Statement directed at that particular sensation or emotion.

4 Follow that assessment with your new Set-Up Statement. Start by repeating three times while tapping the Karate Chop: 'Even though I have this [Mrs Brown sadness], I deeply and completely love and accept myself.'

5 Follow this by tapping the Tapping Sequence using the Reminder Phrases 'this sadness' or variations, 'Mrs Brown sadness' or 'This huge sadness' or 'This sadness in my throat' on each of the eight points (see pages 20–21).

You will enjoy the world from a new perspective
when you are free of your old emotional baggage.

6 Tap through all the aspects that manifest until each is reduced down to a comfortable level and you can run the entire movie in one go without getting any charge. At this point it may seem like you are watching someone else in that situation, it might turn into black and white, or it may have moved very far away. Sometimes you may not be able to see it at all anymore. It will not make what happened OK, but it will prevent you from feeling the pain of it in your life today.

If you work through one or possibly two of these memories (or movies) a day, in a couple of months you will feel significantly different and you will notice an increase in your emotional and physical well-being that goes hand in hand with releasing the negative charge that you may have been carrying around for years.

Programme for change

HEAL THE PAST

- Decide what emotional baggage you would like to be rid of
- Buy a beautiful notebook
- Create a list of movies (see page 55)
- Work with one or two movies a day
- After a one month period, check in with the original emotional baggage and notice what has changed
- Continue as needed.

TOP TAPPING TIPS – HEAL THE PAST

IF YOUR FEELINGS BECOME MORE INTENSE, KEEP TAPPING

The temptation is to stop tapping if intense emotions show up. People often think that the tapping is making them worse. Absolutely not – you are just accessing a deeper layer, which is offering itself for healing. KEEP TAPPING until the emotions have calmed down. Match your tapping to the intensity of the emotions, gradually slowing it down as they release.

USE MOVIE DETAILS INSTEAD OF THE 0–10 SCALE

When using the Movie Technique, check on the changes in the composition of the movie after tapping, instead of using the 0–10 scale. Changes always indicate a shift in your emotions of some form, and that the tapping is working. For example: the movie may turn black and white rather than colour, it may move further away, it may be fuzzy and unclear, or it may be very clear and sharp.

CONTINUALLY TAP ON YOUR FINGER POINTS WHILE SETTING UP YOUR MOVIE

Continually tapping while writing your list of memories and setting your movies up allows your energy system to rebalance all the time, even when you are not formally doing rounds of EFT. This can clear some of the anxiety or fear you may have about doing the process itself, or about revisiting your uncomfortable memories.

Case study – Jack

Jack was in his mid 70s and suffered from high blood pressure. He was on medication and his doctor wanted to increase the dose substantially as it was having little effect.

He was also subject to violent angry outbursts that seemed to come out of nowhere. He had always had a temper but it was getting increasingly worse as he grew older. This was making his home life miserable and his wife of 40 years was threatening to leave him unless he went to see a psychotherapist, which he absolutely did not want to do.

In his words 'I don't want to spend hours sitting talking to someone I don't know and who doesn't know me about my past, raking things over and dredging things up that were over long ago and that I would forget'. This is a very common response to talk therapies, and the reason some people will never seek help. The tapping seems to provide a solution to this. While it is usually necessary to work through past memories, doing this while tapping seems to be a quicker, less painful way of doing so. We are not our stories, although we think we are. What we are tapping on is our body's response to the memories, we don't need to share the content with anyone, not even a practitioner if you choose to work with one. All that is necessary is that you are tuned into what happened to you, and you can keep that completely private. This is one of the joys of the tapping, and one of the reasons it can be so effective in a group – no one needs to share anything if they don't want to.

WHAT DID HE DO?

Having read about EFT he decided to have a go tapping himself. He started by working directly on his blood pressure and got a slight reduction almost immediately. However, the anger remained as before. He tried to analyze what the root cause was but drew a blank. He asked himself questions such as 'When was the first time I felt like this?' He got a sense that it was early in his life, but no specific memory came to mind at this point. So he decided to begin doing a Personal Peace Procedure on all the times he had exploded with this uncontrollable rage. He wrote a list of all the memories he had where his anger had seemed out of control, going back many decades to his early childhood. There were hundreds of episodes!

Far from being discouraged, Jack took this as a challenge and began to work through the memories one by one, starting with the earliest he could remember. His early childhood had been spent in Windsor during the Second World War; he vividly remembered one particular night on which Windsor was bombed when he was about five years old. The next morning he was told that his school had been destroyed and he would not be able to go there anymore. He loved his school and felt very angry. That night bedtime came and he was terrified that more bombs would be dropped. He couldn't sleep and had a massive tantrum that resulted in his being allowed to share his mother's bed and being safe and comforted.

He decided to start here, breaking the memory into a series of mini movies that he named: Night time bombing movie, School bombing movie, Bedtime fear movie, Bedtime anger movie. He then rated the intensity of each of these movies on a scale of 0–10 and noted how that intensity felt in his body.

Then he tapped on each separate movie using Set-Up Statements such as these:

- 'Even though I have this night time bombing terror movie, I deeply and completely love and accept myself'.
- 'Even though I have this bedtime anger movie, I deeply and completely love and accept myself'.
- 'Even though I have this night time bombing anger, I deeply and completely love and accept myself'.

He continued tapping the Sequence points using phrases such as:

- 'Night bombing movie'
- 'That noise'
- 'That terrifying noise'
- 'Night bombing movie'
- 'Bedtime anger movie'
- 'I was so angry'
- 'I was so scared'
- 'Bedtime anger movie.'

DEEPER INTO THE PROCESS

Jack continued to tap on all the different aspects that showed up, and on his emotional response to each of them, until he was able to run the entire memory without any emotional upset or disturbance, and the intensity was close to 0. At this point he used his Heart Anchor, holding the points while running the memory through his mind. He found that he was able to think about the episode from a more objective adult standpoint, as opposed to through the eyes of a five-year-old boy, He then tested his work once more by running the movie while checking for any physical reaction. There wasn't any.

Jack recorded his results in his notebook and set about working on the next memory he had put down. The results were the same, although this time it felt a little quicker.

Over the next six weeks, Jack took a couple of memories a day and worked through them in this way. He expanded his work to tapping through any painful memory that still carried a charge for him in the present day. As he did this he noticed that memories he had originally expected to be of a high intensity seemed to be clearing even before he had turned his attention to them with the tapping.

HOW LIFE CHANGED

During this time he had a couple of appointments with his doctor to check on his blood pressure with a view to upping the medication. To his doctor's surprise and Jack's delight, his blood pressure had dropped dramatically, to such an extent that the doctor actually began to reduce his medication instead. As Jack was feeling so much fitter physically, he was able to do more and took up playing golf and going for walks. His wife was amazed at his new lease of life, and delighted that his angry outbursts seemed to have subsided too.

Chapter 5

COPE WITH STRESS, ANXIETY & DEPRESSION

'Using tapping as a tool to lower your stress threshold means that you are less likely to experience anxiety or depression.'

Reset your stress threshold

Everyone experiences stress, anxiety or depression at some point in their lives. In fact, all three are closely related, often go together and can be difficult to tell apart. Sometimes we just know that we don't feel good and would very much like to feel better! Using EFT regularly can help you reset your stress threshold so you are less likely to experience anxiety or depression.

Our bodies are designed to deal with a certain amount of stress. Stress is a normal response to everyday life, and the avalanche of neurochemicals released in response to a stressful event usually translate into the motivation to take action to resolve a problematic issue. Doing so gives us a sense of satisfaction, then our bodies return to a state of peace. However, when we are not able to resolve stress-inducing situations (or don't believe we can), anxiety can set in. We may feel powerless, and therefore stressed, which in turn leads to an overwhelming anxiety. Living with anxiety and fear is exhausting and can turn into the chronic shutdown of depression. Stress, anxiety and depression show up in different ways for different people. It's important to ask yourself how you experience it, personally.

Using EFT as a tool to deal with your stress threshold will mean that you are less likely to experience anxiety or depression. It is very empowering to find that you are more capable than you thought and that things that used to bother you don't any more. As a consequence you will have more belief in your own ability to solve the problems that present themselves in everyday life. EFT alone is very useful for mild to moderate cases, or in situations of temporary circumstantial stress, anxiety or depression. With persistence, perhaps over a period of months, it is possible to achieve profound change. EFT can be used alongside medical support even in more severe cases where antidepressants or other medication may be required at least in the short term. It really is a complementary treatment.

HEART ANCHOR
(See pages 43–45 for more information)

How might you use your Heart Anchor for stress, anxiety and depression?
Make a commitment to add three things to your Heart Anchor every day. Maybe you notice the architecture in a busy street in a new way or feel the warmth in someone's greeting. Capture those moments by briefly touching the Heart Anchor points as they occur. You may be amazed at how much there is to appreciate once you start looking!

ASK QUESTIONS AND FACE THE ISSUES

• How do I feel depression/stress/anxiety in my body?

_____

_____

• What exactly am I feeling?

_____

_____

• Who or what is currently bothering me?

_____

_____

• Which memories from my past still bother me?

_____

_____

• When did I learn 'I'm not good enough'?

_____

_____

• Who taught me 'I'm not good enough'?

_____

_____

• When did I decide 'I'm not good enough'?

_____

_____

Exercise: Cope with stress, anxiety and depression

Although in this example of how to use EFT we are using the word 'depression', please substitute the words 'anxiety' or 'stress' wherever or whenever they may be more appropriate for you.

FIRST SEQUENCE

The first thing to ask yourself is 'How do I feel depression (or stress, or anxiety) in my body?' Perhaps you feel it as a heaviness in your shoulders or neck, as a difficulty in breathing or a tightness in your chest. These will be the first places where you should start to apply the tapping. Whatever you notice, rate the intensity of the feeling or sensation on your 0–10 scale. Here is an example of how you might use the tapping and Set-Up Statement around the sensation of tightness in the chest, for instance.

1 Start by repeating three times while tapping the Karate Chop: 'Even though I have this [tightness in my chest], I deeply and completely love and accept myself.'

2 Follow this by tapping the Tapping Sequence using the Reminder Phrase 'Tightness in my chest' or variations 'Tightness in my chest because I feel anxious' or 'I feel so anxious' or simply 'Tightness' on each of the eight tapping points (see pages 20–21). While saying the phrase aloud, tap 5–7 times on each point. Focus on any physical sensations that arise in your body.

3 After one round, evaluate the intensity of your feelings on your 0–10 scale now, after the tapping, noting any change.

Tightness in my chest because I feel anxious

Tightness in my chest because I feel anxious

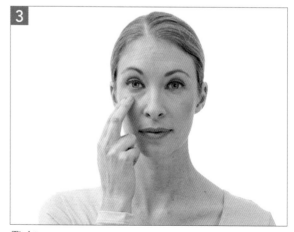

Tightness

Anxious tightness

Difficult to breathe tightness

I feel so anxious

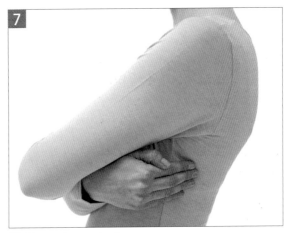

Tightness in my chest

Anxious tightness

4 Now scan your body to see what else you can tap on. Other examples might be tension in the neck, or nervousness in the stomach. For example, if you feel tension in your neck, continue by repeating three times while tapping the Karate Chop: 'Even though I have this [tension in my neck], I deeply and completely love and accept myself.' Follow this by tapping the Tapping Sequence using the Reminder Phrase 'tension in my neck' on each of the eight points (see pages 20–21) while focusing on the feeling of it in your body.

Or if you feel nervousness in your stomach, continue by repeating three times while tapping the Karate Chop: 'Even though I have this [nervousness in my stomach], I deeply and completely love and accept myself.' Follow this by tapping the Tapping Sequence using the Reminder Phrase 'this nervousness in my stomach' on each of the eight tapping points (see pages 20–21) while focusing on the feeling of it in your body.

SECOND SEQUENCE

To continue, ask yourself, 'What exactly am I feeling?' Is it sadness, perhaps? Now create Set-Up Statements that incorporate how you are feeling at this particular moment. Maybe the word 'heaviness' fits with the way you feel at the moment. Let's use that as an example for a Tapping Sequence.

1 Start by repeating three times while tapping the Karate Chop: 'Even though I feel this [heavy sadness right now], I deeply and completely love and accept myself.'

2 Follow this by tapping the Tapping Sequence using the Reminder Phrases 'this sadness' and 'this heavy sadness' on each of the eight points (see pages 20–21). While saying the phrase aloud tap 5–7 times on each point.

THIRD SEQUENCE

Another thing that you can do for yourself with EFT is to consider all the specific events happening around you that cause you to feel uncomfortable at this particular moment. Perhaps you have some uncomfortable situations in your work environment or in your relationships. Work with these by constructing a mini movie (see pages 33–34) in your mind of an experience you have had and then tap through all the feelings and aspects that go with that particular mini movie, which represents something that is happening in your life now.

For instance, many people feel overwhelmed when they arrive in the morning at their place of work, turn on their computer and see all the urgent emails they have to deal with. Here is a simple but effective example showing how to deal with this kind of thing.

QUICK SUMMARY

- To recap, first work out how the physical symptoms of depression, stress or anxiety manifest in your body, then create Set-Up Statements that simply 'tell it as it is' and apply the tapping, remembering to assess the intensity of your feelings before and after you complete the Tapping Sequence.
- Don't forget to vary the phrases – in mid-sequence if necessary – to match how you are actually feeling, if you need to. The important thing is to get more and more adept at noticing what is happening in your body, your thoughts and your feelings.
- When you have cleared some of the physical manifestations of the issue it is often easier to get at the emotions that underpin the physical feelings.

Regular tapping can help to clear the oppressive sadness that is often associated with stress, anxiety and depression.

1 First, visualize a computer screen full of emails, then push the screen away so that you can view it from a comfortable distance; perhaps the screen will be on the wall on the opposite side of the room, or somewhere else 'over there', in the distance. Notice how the intensity of your feelings reduces when you move the picture away like that.

2 Next repeat three times while tapping the Karate Chop: 'Even though I have this email overwhelm, I deeply and completely love and accept myself.'

3 Follow this by tapping the Tapping Sequence while saying your Reminder Phrases aloud and tapping 5–7 times on each of the eight points (see pages 20–21). Vary the words to suit how you are feeling and to describe your particular physical sensations. For example, you might use a selection of the following phrases:

- 'Email overwhelm'
- 'In my head'
- 'I've had enough'
- 'Go away all of you'
- 'Email overwhelm'
- 'Email overwhelm'
- 'Emails in my head!'
- 'Leave me alone!'

4 Keep tapping until you feel more comfortable, assessing your progress on the 0–10 scale. Then when you are ready (that is, when the intensity of your feelings has reduced on the scale) move on to the next stage.

5 Bring the 'email overwhelm' image closer to you and repeat the Set Up and the

Tapping Sequence, as necessary, until you feel comfortable with the email image directly in front of you.

6 Finally, test the method in front of the actual computer screen, tapping as required.

Once you begin to feel a little bit better and clearer about what is happening in your current life, make a list of all the past events that still trouble you today (also see the Movie Technique, pages 33–4, and the Personal Peace

Make a list of all past events that still trouble you today.

Procedure, pages 54–5). Why is it important to do this? Because these memories often signal points in time when something significant happened in our life, or we made a momentous decision, which then created the beliefs that formed the blueprint for our future experiences.

In the case of June (see pages 72–77), we see the power of identifying beliefs that are hidden in the past and releasing them using EFT. By doing this yourself, you can systematically work through all the past events in your life. If you take as little as ten minutes a day to work through one or two troubling memories, you will begin to experience feelings of emotional and physical well-being after a period of two to four weeks. These feelings are the natural result of releasing the negative charges that have been held in your system for an extended period of time.

TOP TAPPING TIPS – COPE WITH STRESS, ANXIETY & DEPRESSION

TAP ON POSSIBILITY

As the intensity begins to reduce it can be useful to introduce the possibility of another way of being: 'Even though I still have some of X, I am open to the possibility I can change now'.

TAP FOR SUBCONSCIOUS CONFLICTS

'Even though I don't want to…'
'Even though I want to, I don't want to…'
'Even though I don't want to, I do want to…'
'Even though part of me refuses to…'

TAP TO FIND INNER PEACE

Tap while saying the beautiful 'Serenity Prayer'

Grant me the serenity
To accept the things I cannot change
Courage to change the things I can,
And the wisdom to know the difference.

Programme for change

COPE WITH STRESS, ANXIETY & DEPRESSION

- Identify physical feelings and clear them
- Identify emotions and clear them
- Work through all feelings about any current situations
- Work through past memories
- Work with your Heart Anchor to appreciate the positives in life.

By tapping to change your response to stressful life situations you will reduce the symptoms of anxiety and depression, too.

Case study – June

Throughout her life June had been prone to periods of stress, anxiety and depression. She described herself as having always been shy and finding things hard to do.

She felt she had to try very hard to keep up in life – as if it was all one big performance – and she was continually being tested and judged. She also felt exhausted a lot of the time; her sleep wasn't good, and as the mother of three children she always felt out of her depth as their development continually brought new challenges.

While she knew that she had changed and developed over the years, she never felt good enough to deal with life in the moment. She had been prescribed antidepressants in the past but disliked the way they made her feel. She had come across EFT when her GP said she had found it 'surprisingly' good for stress. June had found it immediately beneficial when she had applied it to 'stomach butterflies' when speaking to her sister on the phone, and had learned more about it, feeling inspired that she might have found something to help with her problems.

WHAT DID SHE DO?

First June began to notice whenever tension showed up in her body. She started to notice how it related to something she had to do or perhaps to a specific person. She realized that it was always a sign of some kind of stress, anxiety or depression. She actually had to relearn this as she had become very cut off from her body and wasn't able to get its messages clearly at first. The butterflies in her stomach were the first thing she really noticed and then she began to realize how often that type of thing was happening. Whenever she noticed she would tap, first assessing the intensity rating on a scale of 0–10 and using Set-Up Statements such as:

- 'Even though I feel butterflies in my stomach at the thought of speaking to my sister, I deeply and completely love and accept myself.'

Then she continued to tap the Sequence points using her voice to give the right kind of emphasis to phrases such as:

- 'Butterflies in my stomach at the thought of speaking to my sister'
- 'Butterflies in my stomach at the thought of speaking to her'
- 'Butterflies'
- 'Anxious butterflies'
- 'She makes me feel so anxious'
- 'Anxious at the thought of speaking to her'
- 'I just DO NOT want to speak to her.'

It was really important for June to get just the right words that expressed her experience in the moment. Usually she would find that after a few rounds of tapping the intensity would diminish and quite often the physical sensation would actually move! Butterflies in the stomach might become tightness in the throat (see Chasing the Pain technique, pages 36–7). She also found that an emotion or an insight might emerge. The example of her tapping as above actually led to a feeling of sadness (rated as 7), which June then tuned into with the Set-Up Statement:

- 'Even though I have this feeling of sadness, I deeply and completely love and accept myself.'

Followed by tapping on each of the Sequence points:

- 'This sadness.'

After one round, the intensity dropped right down and June had the thought 'I really wish I did want to speak to my sister', followed by the insight that the ongoing conflict with her sister was actually one big stress factor in her life that she just took as normal, to be expected. She began to wonder what it would be like to have a better relationship with her sister.

June also became fascinated to see how using EFT seemed to be reconnecting her with her body. She felt as though she was finally 'getting to know' herself. Around this time she also tentatively began trying out the Heart Anchor for herself. She had avoided it up to this point, thinking that it wouldn't work for her, but found it quite easy to do. She started looking around for things to add to it and was surprised how many pleasant, beautiful or good things there were around her.

She also noticed, that whereas she had always thought she was simply afraid of everything, in fact different things or situations actually brought up different physical sensations in her body. The following are examples of what she noticed and then incorporated into her tapping phrases at different times:

- 'Tension in my neck'
- 'Tight knot in my shoulders'
- 'Red heat in my chest'
- 'Heaviness in my heart'
- 'Constriction in my breathing'
- 'Ball of anger in my stomach.'

As she became more experienced June found that it wasn't always necessary to begin with a formal Set-Up Statement, repeated three times. Quite often she followed her own intuition to leave it out and still got results simply by tapping on the Sequence points. If nothing seemed to happen then she would go back a step and put it in again.

June continued her work by identifying current situations that were bothering her. Over a two-week period she made mini movies (see pages 33–34) in her mind of all the following, and then tapped through the feelings, thoughts, self-talk and body sensations connected to them:

- A difficult meeting with her boss
- The dreaded phone conversation with her sister
- Embarrassment about holding up traffic while trying to park
- Feeling panicky about her husband going away on a business trip
- Looking at her daughter and worrying she would have the same problems.

Doing this allowed her to become much more aware of the emotions underlying the now familiar physical feelings she had been experiencing in her body. And while she was becoming much more aware of feelings of sadness and even anger emerging, at the same time she noticed she felt better in herself, emotionally and physically. She had more energy, a better appetite and was sleeping well for the first time in a very long time. June realized she had spent a lot of time just feeling emotionally numb.

DEEPER INTO THE PROCESS

As June continued to tap through all the emotions, feelings, thoughts and 'the sayings of the internal critical voice' she had noticed, it began to dawn on her that she was living with some very negative beliefs about herself:

- 'I am not good enough.'
- 'I am not loveable enough.'
- 'No one listens to me.'

A major turning point came as she wondered if what she had been believing about herself was really true. So she asked herself the following questions:

- 'When did I learn "I am not good enough"?'
- 'Who taught me "I am not loveable enough"?'
- 'When did I decide "No one listens to me"?'

Relevant memories began to emerge from particular places, times and people in the past. She sat down to write out her list of memories to work through her Personal Peace Procedure (see pages 54–55). Immediately she was able to come up with several memories with an intensity rating of 8 or more. She gave each one a title that summed up its emotional content. She chose 'Too Big For Your Boots' (Intensity 10) since this was a phrase uttered by a teacher to her when she was a small girl, which still had a powerful emotional charge. She worked through it first as a mini movie (see pages 33–34), beginning with the Set-Up Statement: 'Even though I have this "Too Big For Your Boots" movie, I deeply and completely love and accept myself.' She continued by tapping on the Sequence points while repeating the Reminder Phrases 'This "Too Big For Your Boots" movie' and 'These "Too Big for your Boots" emotions'.

This simple approach reduced the intensity of the feelings surprisingly quickly and then June was able to run through the complete memory (lasting about two minutes) as if she was watching a movie in her mind's eye, while continuing to tap. As the remaining intensity reduced, June began to have new insights:

- 'No wonder I decided I was no good!'
- 'He shouldn't have said that – I was just a child doing my best!'
- 'I deserved better than that!'

At the same time feelings of compassion for the younger June and for the teacher involved in the memory began to come through. From this point on June realized that what she had undoubtedly believed about herself were not truths and she no longer had to live as if they were. She could make new choices.

HOW THINGS CHANGED

June began to have much more confidence in herself. She made new friends and began to really enjoy being with people. Those who knew her from before wondered what had happened and someone asked if she had won the lottery. As she became more confident and outgoing she experienced much less stress and anxiety. In her own words 'the most empowering thing for me is that I now know how to release stress and anxiety for myself. If I even get a hint of my old ways these days I know how to deal with it, and I know there is really no need to suffer depression again.'

She felt confident she would be able to deal with whatever presented itself in the future because she had become much more attuned to the internal messages coming from her own body – the physical sensations that gave her an early warning that something was not right – often before her mind had consciously registered a problem. Whenever she noticed one of these warning signals she would take a minute or two to tap, using phrases such as these:

- 'Tightness in my throat.'
- 'Nervousness in my chest about what I have to do... so much to do..too much to do.'

She also learned to moderate how much she took on as a consequence of listening to her body's signals.

June also continued to develop her Heart Anchor. Whenever she noticed thoughts beginning with 'I can't ...' or 'I don't want to...' she took the opportunity to connect to her Heart Anchor and ask: 'Is that really true?' She was able to use the kind of thoughts that in the past would have triggered stress, to connect with her deeper wisdom.

Chapter 6

RELIEVE PHYSICAL PAIN

'Even seemingly constant unremitting pain can be relieved through tapping, often permanently. It is possible to become your own 'aspirin' by tapping in the moment to reduce discomfort.'

Tapping to relieve pain

Before starting to apply tapping to physical pain, it is imperative that you consult your medical practitioner to determine the organic cause of any pain you are experiencing and obtain an appropriate medical diagnosis and possible treatment. Pain is a signal from the body that something is not right; it needs to be respected and treated with sense and caution. EFT can be used very happily alongside any mainstream medical procedure – it is the ultimate complementary therapy in this way.

Whether there is an obvious medical diagnosis or not, it is perfectly possible to get dramatic results in the intensity of pain, both chronic and acute. A curious phenomenon of EFT is that even seemingly constant unremitting pain can be relieved through tapping, often permanently. However, the subconscious mind will not allow total freedom from a pain which has a positive purpose for the body, such as the pain of a broken leg; a degree of pain will remain as a reminder to prevent us doing further damage.

Long-term aches and pains are the bane of many doctors' lives and can be easily and often permanently cleared with the tapping. At the very least, it is possible to become your own 'aspirin' by tapping in the moment to reduce any discomfort.

In our training sessions, we suggest people try it on anything, even symptoms that have a definite cause, such as a slipped disc. While there are no guarantees, people are constantly surprised at the effects of tapping on physical symptoms, especially when these never return.

There are three simple rules to follow when beginning to work with physical pain (see page 80). Very often, following these alone will get significant results.

HEART ANCHOR
(See pages 43–45 for more information)

How might you use your Heart Anchor to deal with pain?
Think of a time when you felt the most relaxed ever. Vividly imagine it as if you were there now. Hear any sounds that go with it and enjoy the feelings. If you touch the Heart Anchor points when the sights, sounds and feelings reach a peak, you will capture the qualities of that time to keep in your heart. It is very difficult to feel relaxation and pain at the same time.

ASK QUESTIONS AND FACE THE ISSUES

- Tuning into the physical, whereabouts in your body do you feel this pain specifically?

_____

_____

_____

_____

_____

- What quality does the pain have?

_____

_____

_____

_____

_____

- On a scale of 0–10, how intense is the pain NOW?

_____

_____

_____

_____

_____

Three simple rules for working with physical pain

RULE 1
Identify the specific location of the pain

When we think about our pains and aches we tend to refer to them in very generalized ways, such as back pain, headache, neck pain and so on. With EFT, we need to be more specific than this to get the maximum effect. We need to identify exactly where we feel the pain. For example, instead of back pain it might be 'this pain at the tip of my left shoulder blade' or 'this pain at the base of my spine'. Identifying the location precisely gives an instruction to your brain and the energy system as to exactly where to apply the healing effects of the tapping.

RULE 2
Describe the quality of the pain

Most pains have a quality: they can be sharp, intermittent, constant, irritating, hot, cold and so on. What is it for you? How would you describe it to someone else? We might use a word like throbbing to add to our example above: 'this throbbing pain on the tip of my left shoulder blade'. Is the word 'pain' exactly right? Or is it an ache, irritation, sore, hurt? They are all different. Is it nagging, irritating, stabbing, dull, angry? It is worth taking time to work out the perfect words for you – you will save time in the long run! So now, our example might be: 'this throbbing ache on the tip of my left shoulder blade'.

RULE 3
Measure the intensity of the pain

Once you have established the location and the quality of the pain, you need to assess the intensity on our scale of 0–10 (see pages 24–25) as it is right now, not how it was yesterday or how it might be tomorrow. The number you give it relates to the intensity of the feeling on the 0–10 scale just before you begin the tapping. Make a note of this, as you will want to refer back to it as you monitor your progress. So our final Set-Up Statement might be: 'Even though I have this throbbing ache on the tip of my left shoulder blade, I deeply and completely love and accept myself.'

Be specific: when tapping to relieve physical pain, work on one symptom at a time, not the whole bunch.

Exercise 1: Relieve physical pain

Using the Set-Up Statement example from our rules, we will begin to tap through the pain.

1 Start by repeating three times while tapping the Karate Chop: 'Even though I have this [throbbing ache on my left shoulder blade], I deeply and completely love and accept myself.'

2 Follow this by tapping the Tapping Sequence using the Reminder Phrases 'this throbbing ache on my left shoulder blade' and 'this throbbing ache' and so on, on each of the eight points (see pages 20–21). While saying the phrase aloud, tap 5–7 times on each point. Take time to tune in to the specific physical sensations on each point, as described by the words you are using. Match your voice to the intensity of your feeling.

3 After a couple of rounds take a deep breath and then check in with the pain. Is it still as intense? Is the quality the same? Is the location the same? These are our three measures for testing results (see page 80).

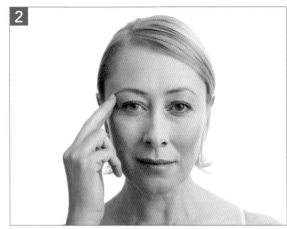

This throbbing ache just there

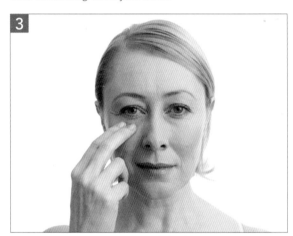

This throbbing ache on my left shoulder blade

This throbbing ache on my left shoulder blade

This throbbing ache just there

This throbbing ache on my left shoulder blade

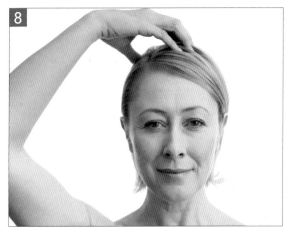

This throbbing ache just there

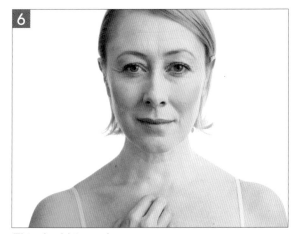

This throbbing ache

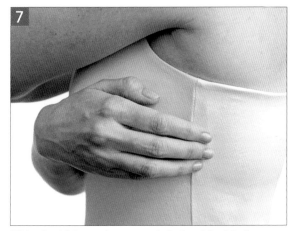

This throbbing ache on my left shoulder blade

Surprisingly, pains can move around the body. If you notice any changes at this point then alter your wording accordingly (as per the instructions above). Follow the pain, wherever it is showing up for you. For more information on the Chasing the Pain Technique, see pages 36–37; pain moving around is so common with tapping that this specific EFT technique has been devised to deal with the phenomenon.

Once you have assessed these three measures you may need to create a new Set-Up Statement, assuming that there has been change in one or other of these areas. In our example, perhaps the throbbing ache is now a dull ache.

4 Continue by repeating your new Set-Up Statement three times while tapping the Karate Chop: 'Even though I have this [dull ache on my left shoulder blade], I deeply and completely love and accept myself.'

5 Follow this by tapping the Tapping Sequence using the Reminder Phrases 'this dull ache on my left shoulder blade' and

'this dull ache' on each of the eight points (see pages 20–21). On each point, take time to tune in to the specific physical sensations as described by the words you are using. Match your voice to the intensity of your feeling.

If you continue to use the Chase the Pain Technique in this way it is quite likely that the pain will disappear altogether. However, you may find yourself stuck, with no movement, change of quality, or reduction in intensity of your physical pain.

Exercise 2: Remove emotional blocks to physical healing

This is the moment to look at how you feel about the pain. It could be that it is the result of an accident and you feel angry, guilty, fearful, sad or something else when you remember what happened. If this is the case, then those feelings may well be interrupting the healing process and you will need to move into working with the emotional aspects that arise.

For example, perhaps you have had a car crash and broken your leg, which is surprisingly slow to heal, according to the doctors. It may be that, if you return to the memory of what happened, you become aware of a feeling of guilt or anger or some similar emotion. Using the Movie Technique (see pages 33–34) to clear any emotional intensity connected to the memory but being felt in the here and now, you may find that the leg begins to heal normally. It seems that our emotions are capable of blocking our healing process, and by addressing them directly with tapping, the body is able to return its attention to the job of physical healing.

It is important to note that the body will not release 'necessary' pains – those needed as a reminder not to cause further injury. However, many of us suffer acute pain at levels that are far more intense than the physical cause would suggest; and these are very real – we are not making them up. By removing the emotional contributors to the pain it will often reduce to a manageable and appropriate level.

EMOTIONS CONNECTED TO PAIN

Ask yourself the following question: if there was an emotion connected to this pain what might it be? Perhaps you will get an answer such as sadness or anger. If that is the case then this is where you switch from focusing on the physical nature of the pain to addressing the possible underlying emotional component that goes with it. So you might continue with:

1 Start by repeating three times while tapping the Karate Chop: 'Even though I have this [sadness], I deeply and completely love and accept myself.'

2 Follow this by tapping the Tapping Sequence using the Reminder Phrases 'this sadness' and 'I feel so sad' on each of the eight points (see pages 20–21). While saying the phrase aloud tap 5–7 times on each point.

Beginning of the eyebrow .... *This sadness*
Side of the eye .... *Feeling so sad*
Under the eye .... *This deep sadness*
Under the nose .... *I feel SO sad*
Chin .... *This sadness*
Collarbone point .... *This deep sadness*
Under the arm .... *I feel so sad*
Top of the head .... *This sadness*

3 Then reassess the intensity of both the physical and emotional feelings on your scale of 0–10. In this way it is possible to address both the physical pain and the underlying emotional components that often go with it. If you ask yourself the question 'If there was an emotion connected to this pain, what would it be?' and find that no answer comes to you, just guess what you would say if you did know. Our experience is that guesses don't come out of nowhere, and continuing to tap with the 'guess' in the same way as outlined in steps 1–3 will often get results, too.

Programme for change
RELIEVE PHYSICAL PAIN

- Tap on immediate presentation of the pain following the three rules: location, quality, and intensity (see page 80)
- Use the Chase the Pain Technique to follow the pain around the body
- If you get stuck, question yourself about emotional contributors to the pain
- Tap through any specific memories that show up.

TOP TAPPING TIPS – RELIEVE PHYSICAL PAIN

TAP ON ANY DOUBTS ABOUT WHETHER EFT WORKS. FOR EXAMPLE, YOUR INTERNAL DIALOGUE MIGHT BE SAYING:
'Even though it won't work for me…'
'Even though nothing ever works for me…'
'Even though tapping only works for other people…'

DESCRIBE THE PAIN
Ask yourself 'If this pain had a shape or a colour, what would it be?', then tap using the shape and colour as describing words in your Set-Up Statement and Reminder Phrases. Notice how these qualities change as you tap.

TAP ON POSSIBILITY
As the intensity of the pain begins to reduce it can be useful to introduce the possibility of another way of being, especially if you have become accustomed to living with physical pain. Try using the following Set-Up Statement: 'Even though I still have some of X, I am open to the possibility that I can change now.'

Case study – Susie

Susie recently had a car accident that had left her with whiplash. Despite many weeks of physiotherapy there was little improvement in her symptoms and she was experiencing a constant dull pain in her neck.

She was taking a large amount of ibuprofen every day and Susie's physiotherapist was surprised by her lack of improvement. She had taught herself EFT previously so decided to use it to see if she could reduce her pain.

WHAT DID SHE DO?

Susie began tapping on the dull neck pain that had an intensity level of 8 (despite the painkillers), using the Set-Up Statement: 'Even though I have this dull neck pain, I deeply and completely love and accept myself .' She continued tapping the Tapping Sequence points using phrases such as 'dull neck pain', 'this dull neck pain', and 'this pain just there'.

After a couple of rounds Susie's pain reduced to a 6 on the 0–10 scale. So she continued to tap using the same words. After a few minutes Susie noticed that the pain had reduced to a score of 4 and that she felt she had a little more mobility. She asked herself: 'How does it feel now?' and checking through our three rules (see page 80) discovered it was more of a pulling sensation on the right side now.

So she continued tapping the points using the Set-Up Statement: 'Even though I have this pulling sensation on the right side of my neck, I deeply and completely love and accept myself.' And again, she tapped the eight points with the Reminder Phrases 'this pulling sensation on the right side of my neck', 'this pulling feeling just there' and 'something pulling on the right side of my neck'.

This reduced to a score of 3, but then, despite changing her words, nothing seemed to happen. So she turned her attention to the accident itself to see whether there was any emotional disruption that needed treating with the tapping.

DEEPER INTO THE PROCESS

Susie thought about the cause of the whiplash – the car accident – and what had happened after, and asked herself how she felt about it. As she remembered it she felt very angry, it hadn't been her fault and she was frustrated that she was still incapacitated from it. She also wanted to 'throttle the insurance companies for all the admin' she was facing. She realized that there were a number of different aspects showing up and tapped on each one as it arose. Some Set-Up Statements that emerged included:

- 'Even though I have this accident anger, I deeply and completely love and accept myself.'
- 'Even though it wasn't my fault, I deeply and completely love and accept myself.'
- 'Even though I am so frustrated, I deeply and completely love and accept myself.'
- 'Even though I want to throttle them, I deeply and completely love and accept myself.'

She continued tapping the Tapping Sequence eight points using phrases such as:

- 'Accident anger'
- 'This anger'
- 'I am so angry'
- 'It wasn't my fault'
- 'Accident anger in my neck'
- 'Feeling frustrated'
- 'This frustration'

- 'I'm so frustrated'
- 'This neck frustration'
- 'I just want to throttle them'
- 'I am so angry'
- 'So frustrated'
- 'I want to throttle them.'

Between each round Susie checked in with the neck pain, as well as the intensity around the specific aspect she was working on. She quickly noticed that she had even more movement and that the pulling sensation had cleared. At the same time her anger had dissipated and she was able to look at the situation from a different perspective – she said she realized she had just been 'in the wrong place at the wrong time'. She also said 'It was just an accident, these things happen!'. This was a total turnaround from how she was feeling before she began tapping.

Then she ran the memory of the accident in her mind, like a mini movie, stopping at any bit that still carried any intensity, and using Set-Up Statements such as:

- 'Even though the car hit me and it was frightening, I deeply and completely love and accept myself.'
- 'Even though he shouted at me, I deeply and completely love and accept myself.'
- 'Even though it made a terrible noise, I deeply and completely love and accept myself.'

She continued tapping the Tapping Sequence eight points using phrases such as:

- 'Car hitting me emotions'
- 'Car hitting me fear'
- 'Car hitting me shock'
- 'The car hit me'
- 'He shouted at me'
- 'His words'
- 'His shouting'
- 'And everything I feel about it'
- 'That noise'
- 'Car hitting me noise'
- 'That terrible noise'
- 'That noise.'

When she was able to rerun the memory from beginning to end with no emotional intensity at all she checked in on the whiplash again but there was no sign of it and she was able to move her neck freely and without any pain. Susie was amazed at her result and felt a burst of joy and empowerment which she added to her Heart Anchor.

HOW LIFE CHANGED

Susie has been free from pain ever since she started tapping and her neck no longer troubles her. She has not needed her painkillers once and her physiotherapist signed her off from treatment. Another positive side effect was that she had dealt with the insurance paperwork easily and was expecting the claim to come through shortly. She felt as fit as she had before the accident happened.

Chapter 7

INCREASE YOUR CONFIDENCE

'With EFT, it is possible to overcome the fears and paralysing symptoms that get in the way of you experiencing genuine confidence in every area of your life.'

Overcome the fear

EFT is a great tool to help you with confidence issues. Most people would like to feel a bit more confidence in some situations while others feel that their fears hold them back in all areas of life. It is possible to overcome the fears and paralysing symptoms that get in the way of you experiencing genuine confidence in every area of your life by using EFT.

Perhaps you would like to have the confidence to approach someone and ask for a date, or to stand up and speak in front of an audience; perhaps you would like to improve your performance in a sport, but you know that nerves are holding you back. Maybe you would like to experience the kind of core confidence in yourself that means you are no longer bothered by the judgements or attitudes of others. True confidence means that you can trust yourself to do the right thing and others will trust and respect you too. People who are genuinely confident are always aware of other people's feelings and have no need to trample on anyone else to get what they want.

Take a moment or two now to consider how your life could improve if you had more confidence. First of all, think about the kinds of situations in which you feel a lack of confidence – especially those where you feel some kind of stress or anxiety, or the physical symptoms of these in your body. Commonly, when we feel nervous or lacking in confidence, we can experience butterflies in our tummy, a tightness in our chest, or a lump in our throat, which makes it difficult for our words to come out clearly.

HEART ANCHOR
(See pages 43–45 for more information)

How might you use your Heart Anchor to gain confidence?
Think of someone you know who really exudes confidence in the way you would like to – maybe a charismatic colleague, or a sports person on TV, for example – and imagine yourself in their shoes. If you immerse yourself in 'being' them just for a moment, and touch the Heart Anchor points at the same time, you can 'borrow' the quality of confidence and keep it in your heart.

ASK QUESTIONS AND FACE THE ISSUES

- How do I know when I am feeling those symptoms of lack of confidence?

_____

_____

_____

_____

_____

- When I feel nervous and anxious where is it showing up in my body?

_____

_____

_____

_____

_____

- When was the first time I felt this feeling in my throat (or other part of the body)?

_____

_____

_____

_____

_____

How do I know when I am feeling the symptoms of lack of confidence?

Often, the best place to begin EFT is with the physical sensations that you experience in your body that go with some kinds of emotional states. For instance, perhaps you feel nervous and anxious about doing an interview. Ask yourself: 'When I feel nervous and anxious where is it showing up in my body?'

Then incorporate the body sensation you have indentified into your Set-Up Statement (see pages 17–19). If you have several physical symptoms, take each one in turn and do a Set-Up Statement then tap the Tapping Sequence

Tap for confidence and discover a new you.

on each, measuring the before and after intensity using our 0–10 scale . The following are examples of possible Set-Up Statements to be said out loud while tapping the Karate Chop three times:

- 'Even though I feel these butterflies in my tummy, I deeply and completely love and accept myself.'
- 'Even though I feel these butterflies just thinking about that interview, I deeply and completely love and accept myself.'
- 'Even though I am so nervous in my gut about the interview, I deeply and completely love and accept myself.'
- 'Even though I can hardly swallow when I think about that, I deeply and completely love and accept myself.'

Then continue by tapping each of the eight points in the Tapping Sequence repeating your Reminder Phrase on each. The Reminder Phrases from our example might be:

- 'I can hardly swallow when I think about that'
- 'Can hardly swallow.'

Or add a variation that also describes what you are experiencing, examples might be:
- 'Feel awful'
- 'I feel so nervous'
- 'Can hardly swallow thinking about it.'

Exercise: Increase your confidence

A complete first round working on a confidence issue might go as follows:

1 Start by repeating three times while tapping the Karate Chop: 'Even though [I can hardly swallow when I think about it], I deeply and completely love and accept myself.'

2 Follow this by tapping the Tapping Sequence using the Reminder Phrase 'I can hardly swallow' on each of the eight points (see pages 20–21). While saying the phrase aloud tap 5–7 times on each point.

3 Assess the intensity on your 0–10 scale after one full round, then continue to do as many rounds as you need to, adjusting the words where necessary, until you begin to feel more comfortable in your body. Next, start to think about the actual situation that is troubling you. Perhaps it is an interview, perhaps it is going to a party, perhaps it is needing to tell somebody something important and you are afraid that they won't accept what you have to say.

I can hardly swallow when I think about that

Feel awful

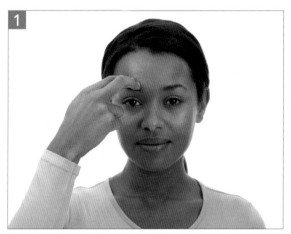

I can hardly swallow when I think about that

I feel so nervous

I can hardly swallow when I think about that

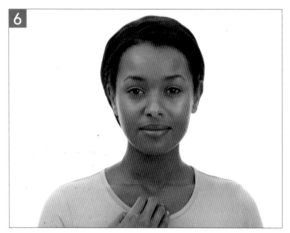

Can hardly swallow

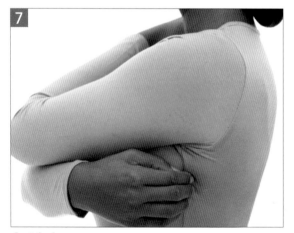

Just feel so nervous

I can hardly swallow when I think about that

4 Make a mini movie of the scenario that you are already imagining and which has been creating these physical responses in your body, and then tap through each of the frames covering all the aspects. For instance, you might want to give the whole thing a title, like 'The Interview' and then you would begin tapping and repeating your Set-Up Statement three times while tapping the Karate Chop: 'Even though [I have "The Interview" emotions], I deeply and completely love and accept myself.

5 Then tune your mind into the beginning point of the movie – perhaps it is you opening the door and walking into a room full of strangers. Hold the scene in your mind's eye and tap while you are tuning in to it. Tap the Tapping Sequence using the Reminder Phrases on each of the eight points (see pages 20–21).

Beginning of the eyebrow ....*I can see them looking at me*
Side of the eye .... *I know everybody is looking at me*
Under the eye..............*I won't know who to talk to*
Under the nose...............................*I feel so stupid*

Chin.................................. *I know I'll feel nervous*
Collarbone point ....*I'll be looking for someone to talk to*

Under the arm ....*No one will want to talk to me*
Top of the head .... *I just won't know what to say*

6 And then keep tapping through repeated sequences until you can think about that potential scenario, the mini movie, while feeling comfortable in your body.

Sometimes it might just take a couple of rounds of tapping to achieve a positive change. At other times you might need to do more. If you consistently tap through all of the experiences that cause you to feel a lack of confidence until you are able to think about them in a relatively comfortable way, you will find your actual experiences will be more comfortable too. That is how EFT works.

Programme for change

INCREASE YOUR CONFIDENCE

- Begin with physical sensations – where do I feel this in my body?
- Clear away any emotions you are feeling or that emerge as you tap on the physical sensations you experience
- Work through associated memories
- Work through imaginary scenarios
- Constantly test your progress.

TOP TAPPING TIPS – INCREASE YOUR CONFIDENCE

KEEP CHECKING IN WITH YOURSELF
Continually check your words and your breathing. If you feel a shift, stop and check what is happening for you. Allow the shifts to occur without interpretation – just follow where your body and mind lead you next.

GO FOR GOLD!
Tap for what you really want, not what you think you should want, or could get. We really don't know what is possible, but miracles happen every day. Do you deserve a miracle?

SET A SPECIFIC GOAL AND TAP WHILE VIVIDLY IMAGINING YOURSELF ACHIEVING IT
If you are unable to visualize, tap on the Set-Up Statement 'Even though I can't quite see it yet, I deeply and completely love and accept myself.'

Case study – Dinah

Dinah was recently promoted at work and at first she was delighted that her hard work and talents had been recognized. Then her excitement turned to anxiety when she realized her new position would require her to speak in public.

In her new role, Dinah would be expected to give presentations and speak to large groups of people. Yet public speaking was her worst nightmare!

She realized she had done everything in her power in the past to avoid any such situation – to such an extent that she had even forgotten she had this problem. Now everything came right back to her. In fact Dinah felt so bad at the prospect of public speaking that she was not even able to create a mini movie of a future scenario. The following demonstrates how Dinah used EFT to clear the fears that were getting in the way of her even being able to think about speaking, and then to remove any remaining blocks to her creating a positive visualization of her self succeeding in a way she had never thought possible.

WHAT DID SHE DO?

As soon as Dinah started thinking about the prospect of public speaking she noticed a very distinct 'painful, flipping sensation' in her 'tummy'. This was the obvious place to begin tapping. Dinah rated the intensity as a full 10 on the 0–10 scale and began tapping on the Karate Chop three times with the Set-Up Statement 'Even though I have this painful, flipping sensation in my tummy, I deeply and completely love and accept myself.' Then Dinah continued tapping the Tapping Sequence points using the Reminder Phrase 'this painful, flipping sensation in my tummy' while concentrating on her physical sensations.

After two rounds the intensity level dropped from 10 to 7 on the scale, and then from 7 to 4. At this point the painful flipping sensation had actually gone and the 4 intensity related to 'a lumpy, gripping feeling' in her throat. She created a new Set-Up Statement, slightly varying the words in each of the three repetitions:

- 'Even though I have this lumpy, gripping feeling in my throat, I deeply and completely love and accept myself.'
- 'Even though I feel this lumpy, gripping feeling in my throat just thinking about it, I deeply and completely love and accept myself.'
- 'Even though something's gripping my throat, I accept myself completely.'

Dinah then repeated the process, tapping the eight points, using Reminder Phrases such as these at each point:

- 'This lumpy, gripping feeling in my throat'
- 'Lumpy, gripping feeling just thinking about it'
- 'Something gripping my throat.'

DEEPER INTO THE PROCESS

The intensity, however, seemed to stick at 4. At this point Dinah asked herself the question, 'When was the first time I felt this feeling in my throat?' At first nothing came, but then a memory surfaced that seemed to be directly related. She kept on tapping as she literally saw herself, in her mind's eye. What had emerged seemed to be connected to an intense feeling of disappointment in herself, relating to something that had happened at school when she was about seven years old. She clearly remembered getting something wrong at school and being brought to the front of the class by Miss Simpson 'to explain' herself. Under such pressure she couldn't get any words out, her throat tightened and she 'just wanted to die'. She felt attacked.

Now Dinah was able to use the Movie Technique (see pages 33–34) with this memory. She gave it the title 'Miss Simpson Attacked Me', intensity 9 and began tapping with the following Set-Up Statement: 'Even though I have this "Miss Simpson Attacked Me" movie, I deeply and completely love and accept myself.' She then repeated the Reminder Phrase 'This "Mrs Simpson Attacked Me" Movie' on each of the eight points in the Tapping Sequence.

As the intensity reduced from 9 to 7 to 5, Dinah began to see more clearly different aspects. She continued tapping with the following Reminder Phrases working through the different aspects:

- 'She really hurt me'
- 'I couldn't speak out'
- 'I was such a disappointment'
- 'I felt such a failure'
- 'I just wanted to die.'

Then she began to feel really angry about what had happened back then:

- 'She shouldn't have treated me like that'
- 'I feel so angry'
- 'I was just a kid and she treated me like that!'

As Dinah worked through the layers of feelings, the self-blame and disappointment turned to anger at the teacher, and then to compassion for herself. At this point Dinah used her Heart Anchor, holding the points while running the memory through her mind. Now she was actually able to feel compassion for the teacher. At this point Dinah knew she was done with this memory. The Miss Simpson memory no longer had any negative charge for Dinah.

The next stage was to test how she felt about the prospect of public speaking now. To Dinah's surprise, she no longer felt the painful, flipping sensation in her tummy. Now she was able to create in her mind a mini movie of herself speaking in front of a group. She discovered she was able to think through most of the aspects of this future scenario comfortably. She felt most intense about 'people watching' and 'forgetting my words' – both rated 4. A couple of rounds with each of these reduced the intensity down to 0. Then she tried viewing her mini movie while holding the Heart Anchor points and was 'slightly astonished' to find herself enjoying it!

HOW LIFE CHANGED

The final test came when Dinah did her first presentation. In her own words, she was 'absolutely amazed at herself' and had no fear whatsoever.

Dinah used EFT very successfully to work on her own fears about speaking in public. She began by focusing on what was happening for her in the present time whenever she thought about the problem. By using tapping initially on her body symptoms she was able to reduce the intensity of those feelings, which then allowed the next piece of the problem to emerge – the school memory. It is often the case that a feeling (Dinah's throat) in present time is actually connected to something unresolved from the past. Your subconscious wisdom will guide you through this process when you know how to engage with it. Dinah was able to do this at the turning point in her session by asking herself: 'When was the first time I felt this feeling in my throat?'

It is also interesting to note how Dinah's perception shifted as she thought about the teacher while firing the Heart Anchor points. Her emotional response to Miss Simpson changed from anger to compassion. When this happens, we think of it as 'looking through Love's eyes'.

Chapter 8

LOSE WEIGHT

'EFT can bring about healthy weight loss by enabling the individual to eliminate cravings and change their relationship with food.'

The quest for the perfect weight

The majority of overweight people know the basic facts regarding weight loss, the formula of calories in to calories out, and the combination of healthy eating and exercise. They know what to do and how to do it; in fact, they are often the experts. So why is it that people continue to be unsuccessful in their quest for the perfect weight. Why do people continue to yoyo diet, clutching on to each new fad as it appears, only to have their hopes shattered yet again?

The answer is that being overweight is just a symptom of an underlying emotional problem. As with any addiction, overeaters use food to suppress underlying emotional anxieties, whether they are in or out of their conscious awareness. The success of EFT is due to the individual working directly with these anxieties and addressing the deeper thought processes. Unless these are successfully recognized and tackled, the old behaviours around food will continue to sabotage the best intentions and diets. Food is used as anaesthesia, masking emotional discomfort of some form. EFT treats the problem by healing from the inside.

You can work very effectively with weight issues using tapping. The question is where do you start? There are a couple of approaches to using EFT for weight loss that will help you begin your personal journey. Remember, healthy weight loss takes place over a period of time. You are looking to change your lifestyle in order to achieve long-lasting weight loss and let go of the need for diets and the like. While the tapping does get quick results, you are not likely to reach your ideal weight in a matter of days – but if you keep tapping patiently and with persistence you will surprise yourself at how easy it can be.

HEART ANCHOR
(See pages 43–45 for more information)

How might you use your Heart Anchor to deal with weight loss?
Imagine a picture of yourself at your ideal weight; tap to clear any interfering thoughts and feelings. In your mind's eye, put this picture in your heart and add the good feelings that go with it to your Heart Anchor.

ASK QUESTIONS AND FACE THE ISSUES

• If I could never eat one food type again what would I miss the most?

_____

_____

• What food do I crave the most?

_____

_____

• When/where/with whom do I crave it?

_____

_____

• How does the craving feel in my body?

_____

_____

• How do I feel about my weight?

_____

_____

• When was the first time I felt like that?

_____

_____

• What does that remind me of?

_____

_____

Exercise 1: Break the pattern

The first step is to use tapping to interrupt behaviours that create overeating and an unhealthy relationship with food. Apply the tapping to feelings or cravings around food. What is the particular substance that you crave? Is it chocolate? Maybe it is carbs, or bread. Whatever it is, think about the particular thing, assess the intensity of the craving on the scale of 0–10 (see pages 24–25), and begin tapping.

1 Start by repeating three times while tapping the Karate Chop: 'Even though I [crave chocolate/have to have chocolate/am going to have chocolate], I deeply and completely love and accept myself.'

2 Follow this by tapping the Tapping Sequence using the Reminder Phrases on each of the eight points (see pages 20–21). While saying the phrases aloud tap 5–7 times on each point, varying the statements slightly, until the intensity of the craving begins to reduce.

I really crave chocolate

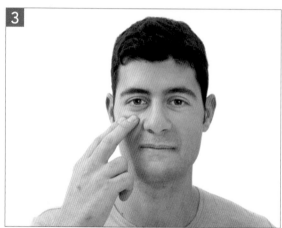

This chocolate craving

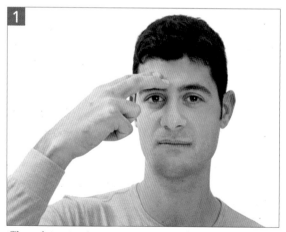

Chocolate craving

I just have to have it

I can't stop craving chocolate

I'm going to have it

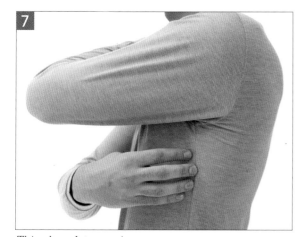

This chocolate craving

This chocolate craving

3 Stop and assess the intensity of the craving again. Has it gone up or down? Occasionally the intensity will go up before reducing. This means that you have accessed a deeper layer of the issue that needs your attention with EFT. How does it feel? Can you connect to any thoughts or emotions?

4 Reformulate a new Set-Up Statement and continue to repeat three times while tapping the Karate Chop: 'Even though [my craving is getting stronger/getting worse], I deeply and completely love and accept myself.'

5 Next tap the Tapping Sequence using variations on the Reminder Phrases below on each of the eight points as before. While saying the phrase aloud tap 5–7 times on each point.

Beginning of the eyebrow .... *This craving*
Side of the eye ....*Getting stronger*
Under the eye........................ *This intense craving*
Under the nose... *I just have to have that chocolate*
Chin .... *This chocolate craving*
Collarbone point .... *Getting worse*
Under the arm .... *Fear of making it worse*
Top of the head .... *I just have to have it*

Exercise 2: Interrupt the routine

To get to the root of a weight issue you need to interrupt the times and places where problematic eating behaviours are most likely to occur. So what is it for you? Maybe you always eat when you come home from work; maybe you always reach for chocolate after you have taken a phone call from a particular person; or perhaps your eating is fairly stable until you have to do a presentation at work. What is your particular ritual?

TIME AND PLACE ISSUES

Once you have this information to hand, create Set-Up Statements around it and tap before you are likely to be in those particular situations. For example, if you know you always have to eat something sugary when you come home from work, then well in advance of that time, you would tap something like this. A complete first round using this method to address an eating issue when getting home from work might be as follows:

1 Start by repeating one of the following phrases three times while tapping the Karate Chop: 'Even though [I have to eat as soon as I get home], I deeply and completely love and accept myself' or 'Even though [I can't stop eating when I get home], I deeply and completely love and accept myself' or 'Even though [I am just not satisfied unless I have chocolate when I get home], I deeply and completely love and accept myself.'

2 Follow this by tapping the Tapping Sequence using the Reminder Phrases below on each of the eight points (see pages 20–21). While saying the phrase aloud, tap 5–7 times on each point.

Beginning of the eyebrow .... *I always eat when I get home*

Side of the eye ..... *It is the time when I get home, that is when I eat*

Under the eye........................ *I always do it when I come straight through the door*

Under the nose.............................. *That's the time*

Chin................................... *That's the problem time*

Collarbone point ....*As soon as I come home from work*

Under the arm ....*That's when I overeat*

Top of the head ....*I always overeat when I come home from work*

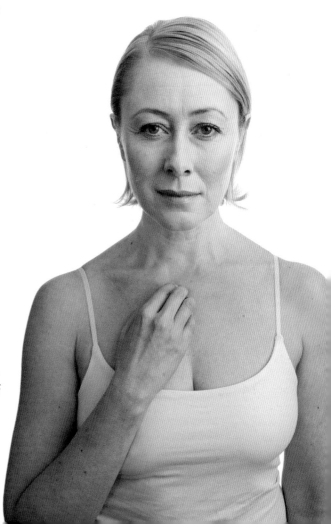

Exercise 3: Understand beliefs

Now take a look at the beliefs you hold concerning your weight. Whenever you have difficulty in changing a behaviour or maintaining that change, it is likely that there is an underlying limiting or conflicting belief operating. Beliefs are not necessarily logical or rational but the result of understandings taken from past experiences, which may not be appropriate today.

Beliefs work from the heart, behaviours from the mind, and our beliefs are very powerful saboteurs in weight loss. Typical limiting beliefs that block success around weight loss are offered in the numerous following Set-Up Statements and Tapping Sequences.

SELF-DOUBT

1 Start by repeating three times while tapping the Karate Chop: 'Even though [I don't believe I can reach my goal weight], I deeply and completely love and accept myself.'

2 Follow this by tapping the Tapping Sequence using the Reminder Phrases below on each of the eight points (see pages 20–21), while saying the phrases aloud tap 5–7 times on each point.

Beginning of the eyebrow .... *I can't reach my goal weight*
Side of the eye ....*It just isn't possible for me*
Under the eye ....*I can't do it*
Under the nose ....*No way*
Chin.......................*I will never reach my goal weight*
Collarbone point .... *It is impossible for me*
Under the arm .... *I will never do it*
Top of the head ....*I can't reach my goal weight*

MAINTAINING THE STATUS QUO

1 Start by repeating three times while tapping the Karate Chop: 'Even though [all my family are fat], I deeply and completely love and accept myself.'

2 Follow this by tapping the Tapping Sequence using the Reminder Phrases below on each of the eight points (see pages 20–21). While saying the phrases aloud tap 5–7 times on each point.

Beginning of the eyebrow .... *All my family are big/large/fat*
Side of the eye .... *I can't be different*
Under the eye .... *We are all this way in my family*
Under the nose .... *It is just how it is for us*
Chin........................*Tapping won't change anything*
Collarbone point ..... *All my family are big/large/fat*
Under the arm .... *It isn't safe to be different*
Top of the head ....*It is just how it is in my family*

SELF-DEFEATING

1 Start by repeating three times while tapping the Karate Chop: 'Even though [I am convinced I will regain the weight again], I deeply and completely love and accept myself.'

2 Follow this by tapping the Tapping Sequence using the Reminder Phrases below on each of the eight points (see pages 20–21). While saying the phrases aloud tap 5–7 times on each point.

Beginning of the eyebrow ....*I will never keep the weight off*
Side of the eye ....*I always put it back on again*
Under the eye ....*I just know it will go on again*
Under the nose ...... *It always goes on again for me*

Chin .... *This time won't be any different*
Collarbone point .... *I can never keep it off*
Under the arm ..... *I always put the weight back on*
Top of the head .... *I can't keep the weight off*

FEAR OF UNHAPPINESS

1 Start by repeating three times while tapping the Karate Chop: 'Even though [I am afraid I will still be unhappy if I lose weight], I deeply and completely love and accept myself.'

2 Follow this by tapping the Tapping Sequence using the Reminder Phrases below on each of the eight points (see pages 20–21). While saying the phrases aloud tap 5–7 times on each point.

Beginning of the eyebrow ....*Fear of still being unhappy*
Side of the eye .... *What if being thin doesn't make me happy?*
Under the eye ....*What if I am still unhappy?*
Under the nose .... *This fear*
Chin ....*Fear of remaining unhappy*
Collarbone point ...*Fear of it not being the solution*
Under the arm . *What if it doesn't make me happy?*
Top of the head .... *What if it does?*

LOW SELF-ESTEEM

1 Start by repeating three times while tapping the Karate Chop: 'Even though [I don't deserve to be thin], I deeply and completely love and accept myself.'

2 Follow this by tapping the Tapping Sequence using the Reminder Phrases below on each of the eight points (see pages 20–21). While saying the phrases aloud tap 5–7 times on each point.

Beginning of the eyebrow .... *I don't deserve to be thin*
Side of the eye ..*Someone like me doesn't deserve to be thin*
Under the eye..............................*I don't deserve it*
Under the nose........ *Being thin is for other people*
Chin............................*I deserve to keep the weight*
Collarbone point .... *I don't deserve success*
Under the arm . *I don't deserve to have what I want*
Top of the head ....*I don't deserve to succeed*

IMPOSSIBLE EXPECTATIONS

1 Start by repeating three times while tapping the Karate Chop: 'Even though [it is not possible for me to be thin], I deeply and completely love and accept myself.'

2 Follow this by tapping the Tapping Sequence using the Reminder Phrases below on each of the eight points (see pages 20–21). While saying the phrases aloud tap 5–7 times on each point.

Beginning of the eyebrow . *It's not possible for me*
Side of the eye .... *I will never do it*
Under the eye...................... *It is impossible for me*
Under the nose.................................*I won't do it*
Chin...............................*It will never happen for me*
Collarbone point ....*It will never be possible for me*
Under the arm ....*It is just not possible for me*
Top of the head ....*I will never do it*

By using EFT to promote healthy weight loss you can achieve physical and emotional lightness and well-being.

Exercise 4: Go deeper

There are a number of very useful questions that you can ask yourself about your weight and eating issues. Read through the following examples and note down which questions provoke a response within you, however slight. That will show you where you should take your tapping next.

- When did you first feel uncomfortable about your weight or the way you look?
- When has it been better, and when worse? What memories do you have connected to these times?
- Fill in the following sentence: 'I have to overeat to feel [safe/accepted/relaxed]'.
- What emotions are you trying to suppress or avoid by overeating/feeling stuffed?
- How aware are you of the physical appearance of other people?
- What kinds of things do you notice about others' physical appearance?
- What are you most critical of?
- How do people close to you view appearance and weight?
- How possible is it for you to lose weight and to maintain the weight loss, for you? For others?
- How possible is it for you to like the way you look?
- What would you be doing if you were free of this?
- What would you have to do if you didn't have this problem?
- What would be different for you if you achieved what you wanted?
- What would be different for people around you if you achieved what you wanted?
- What would be different for the rest of the world if you achieved what you wanted?

Then create Set-Up Statements to address the specific responses you give. The following examples may be helpful.

FEAR OF SOCIALIZING

1 Start by repeating three times while tapping the Karate Chop: 'Even though [I would have to go out more if I was thin], I deeply and completely love and accept myself.'

2 Follow this by tapping the Tapping Sequence using the Reminder Phrases below on each of the eight points (see pages 20–21). While saying the phrases aloud tap 5–7 times on each point.

Beginning of the eyebrow ......*I would have to go out more*
Side of the eye ....*I would have to be seen*
Under the eye.....................*Fear of being out there*
Under the nose.........*Fear of not being able to hide*
Chin...*Fear of being seen*
Collarbone point ....*Fear of being noticed*
Under the arm ....*Fear of being attractive*
Top of the head ....*Fear of getting out there*

DEALING WITH EMOTIONS
Perhaps the thought of truly feeling is frightening for you. If so see below:

1 Start by repeating three times while tapping the Karate Chop: 'Even though [I will have to deal with my emotions if I stop overeating], I deeply and completely love and accept myself.'

2 Follow this by tapping the Tapping Sequence using the Reminder Phrases below on each of the eight points (see pages

20–21), while saying the phrases aloud tap 5–7 times on each point.

Beginning of the eyebrow ....*Fear of how I might feel*
Side of the eye ....*Fear of my emotions*
Under the eye.................. *I don't want to feel them*
Under the nose........................ *It is too frightening*
Chin.............................. *What if I can't handle them*
Collarbone point ....*What if I can?*
Under the arm ....*Fear of my emotions*
Top of the head.......................*Fear of dealing with my emotions*

Or you may be fearful of how someone else might feel if you lost weight.

1 Start by repeating three times while tapping the Karate Chop: 'Even though [my sister would be upset if I lost weight], I deeply and completely love and accept myself.'

2 Follow this by tapping the Tapping Sequence using the Reminder Phrases below on each of the eight points (see pages 20–21). While saying the phrases aloud tap 5–7 times on each point.

Beginning of the eyebrow .... *She would be upset*
Side of the eye .... *Fear of her jealousy*
Under the eye .... *Fear of not belonging*
Under the nose.................... *Fear of losing her love*
Chin..*Fear of hurting her*
Collarbone point .... *Fear of upsetting her*
Under the arm ....*Fear of her jealousy*
Top of the head........................ *Fear of hurting her*

Or perhaps it just doesn't feel safe, for you or for others, to lose weight. You may not know

why that is, but if the idea resonates it is worth tapping as follows:

1 Start by repeating three times while tapping the Karate Chop: 'Even though [it's not safe to lose weight], I deeply and completely love and accept myself.'

2 Follow this by tapping the Tapping Sequence using the Reminder Phrases below on each of the eight points (see pages 20–21). While saying the phrases aloud tap 5–7 times on each point.

Beginning of the eyebrow ....*It is not safe*
Side of the eye .... *I won't be safe if I am thin*
Under the eye......................*It is not safe to be thin*
Under the nose............. *It is not safe for me if I am my ideal weight*
Chin..*It is not safe for others*
Collarbone point ....*It is not safe to be thin*
Under the arm .... *Fear of not being safe*
Top of the head ....*It is just not safe*

Or maybe:

1 Start by repeating three times while tapping the Karate Chop: 'Even though [I might get unwanted attention], I deeply and completely love and accept myself.'

2 Follow this by tapping the Tapping Sequence using the Reminder Phrases below on each of the eight points (see pages 20–21). While saying the phrases aloud tap 5–7 times on each point.

Beginning of the eyebrow .... *Fear of the wrong sort of attention*

Side of the eye ....*Fear of attracting the wrong people*

Under the eye............*Fear of people looking at me*

Under the nose ....*Fearing of being seen*

Chin .... *Fear of being hit on*

Collarbone point ....*Fear of being sexually attractive*

Under the arm .... *Fear of unwanted attention*

Top of the head .... *Fear of being attractive*

Beliefs are not truths, they are merely decisions we made, usually during our childhood, based on things that happened at the time. We treat them as truths and behave accordingly. However, often when we look at them in detail we realize that we are running our lives based on the decisions of a small child!

Look at your beliefs around weight and food. Are they useful to you? How old were you when you made these decisions? What was happening in your life then?

You may find that a memory, or someone in particular, comes to mind. This will not be random, so don't dismiss it – the chances are it will be worth tapping on. Take the memory or image and notice any feelings that are connected to it. Tap to clear it using the Movie Technique (see pages 33–34).

Perhaps you have a memory of not finishing everything on your plate at mealtime when you were a child and of your mother shouting at you. This memory may have led to a compulsion to eat everything in case you get into trouble again, which in turn might create the belief 'I have to eat to keep safe'. Once you have made this decision (subconsciously) you will be driven to act it out. When you bring it into conscious awareness as a result of the tapping and self-enquiry you are then in a position to work on changing it. Once we recognize our underlying beliefs and their origins it is easy to change them with tapping.

So let us work through a complete first round working on a memory using the Movie Technique (see pages 33–34) and zoom into the specific piece of the memory that carries the highest emotional charge:

MOTHER SHOUTING MOVIE

1 Start by repeating three times while tapping the Karate Chop: 'Even though [I have this "mother shouting" movie], I deeply and completely love and accept myself.'

2 Follow this by tapping the Tapping Sequence using the Reminder Phrases below on each of the eight points (see pages 20–21). While saying the phrases aloud tap 5–7 times on each point.

Beginning of the eyebrow ....*Mother shouting movie*

Side of the eye ....*Mother shouting movie*

Under the eye ....*She shouted*

Under the nose........................*I decided I was bad*

Chin................................. *Mother shouting memory and the meanings I gave it*

Collarbone point .... *She shouted*

Under the arm ....*At me!*

Top of the head ....*Mother shouting movie*

Run the memory again in your mind, stopping to tap at any point that still has any emotional intensity, however slight. There may be many memories that come into your awareness as you go through the above questions, and it doesn't matter which one you begin with. However, it is important to write them down and return to them systematically to clear any emotional response showing up in the here and now.

Programme for change
LOSE WEIGHT

- Begin with cravings
- Work through specific times when overeating behaviour shows up
- Clear emotional responses
- Work through associated memories.

TOP TAPPING TIPS – LOSE WEIGHT

TAP ON YOUR OVEREATING RITUALS. WHEN DO YOU OVEREAT? AND WITH WHOM?
'Even though I have to have chocolate after dinner…'
'Even though I always overeat with X…'

TAP FOR SUBCONSCIOUS CONFLICTS
'Even though I don't want to…'
'Even though part of me refuses to…'

TAP ON BLOCKS TO CHANGE DIRECTLY
'Even though something is blocking me from changing this…'
'Even though something is getting in the way of this…'
'Even though I have this block…'

TAP FOR DESERVING ISSUES
'Even though I don't deserve to X…'
'Even though I am not allowed X…'
'Even though I am not good enough for X…'
'Even though people like me don't deserve X…'

USE SOFTENERS
Introduce words such as 'maybe', 'perhaps', 'possibly'. These words begin to bridge the gap between the problem state and the solution.

Tapping will empower you
to transform your relationship
with food and meal times.

Case study – Jane

Jane was in her mid 30s and had been on a constant diet since her early teens. Despite her best efforts she never succeeded in keeping the weight off and now was carrying over 10 kg (22 lbs) of excess weight.

She went to the gym regularly and did not drink alcohol. She felt defeated and desperate. Having read about tapping she decided to give it a go, although she was deeply cynical.

WHAT DID SHE DO?

Jane began by exploring what foods she craved most. She asked herself: 'If I could never eat one food type again what would I miss the most?' The answer was pasta. The thought of never enjoying a bowl of spaghetti again made her feel surprisingly tearful so she began tapping right there using Set-Up Statements such as these:

- 'Even though I have to have pasta, I deeply and completely love and accept myself.'
- 'Even though I feel sad without pasta, I deeply and completely love and accept myself.'
- 'Even though I feel sad at that thought, I deeply and completely love and accept myself.'

Then she continued tapping the points using Reminder Phrases such as:

- 'Pasta sadness'
- 'Have to have sadness'
- 'Missing pasta sadness'
- 'I need pasta.'

The intensity of the sadness quickly reduced and in its place a memory popped up of her mother cooking Jane's favourite pasta dish on a winter's night, and all the family sitting around the table tucking in and having fun making a mess with the pasta. The memory made her feel safe and warm, and she could feel that warmth in her tummy.

As this was a positive feeling for Jane she fired her Heart Anchor points. Now she was able to bring about those feelings of safety and warmth without the need to overeat pasta. She found this fascinating and very empowering. For the first time she had a practical alternative to overeating to help her access these positive states.

DEEPER INTO THE PROCESS

Jane continued to tap a few rounds about her emotional response to pasta, and what it represented for her, and was able to reduce her craving for carbohydrates in general surprisingly quickly. This did not result in her never eating pasta again, merely allowed her the freedom of choice.

She used the statement below:

- 'Even though pasta represents fun and security to me, I deeply and completely love and accept myself.'

Then she continued tapping the points using Reminder Phrases such as:

- 'Pasta emotions'
- 'Pasta safety'
- 'Fear of losing those pasta feelings'
- 'Fear of being deprived of pasta'
- 'Pasta memory'
- 'Everything pasta means to me.'

She continued with:

- 'Even though pasta makes me feel safe and warm inside, I deeply and completely love and accept myself.'

And she continued tapping the points using Reminder Phrases such as:

- 'Needing warmth'
- 'Fear of feeling unsafe'
- 'Fear of losing that warmth'
- 'Fear of losing my comforter.'

When Jane really understood the emotional contributors that surrounded her relationship with food, and how, by using tapping, she could become her own detective and achieve lasting change, she felt both excited and empowered. She set about creating her personal programme of change.

She began by exploring other food cravings in the same way as she had done with the pasta, asking herself questions such as:

- 'How would I feel if I didn't overeat X?'
- 'What does X remind me of?'
- 'How do I feel in my body when I think of losing X?'
- 'What does it mean to me?'

As she worked through one food stuff per day she noticed that she was eating more healthily without having to think about it at all, and she had lost a couple of kilograms effortlessly.

Then she turned her attention to the memories she had that involved food, such as family mealtimes, restaurants and treats. She realized that whenever she felt upset about anything, her mother's way of dealing with it was to give her something sweet to eat to 'raise her blood sugar levels'. She never actually listened to whatever the problem was, and Jane was taking over her mother's mantle when it came to her own emotional well-being. She had learnt the pattern so well from her mother that she had been totally unaware of it, and indeed of the fact that emotions were the reason she was reaching for

the food. It was an automatic conditioned response. So she tapped around the various aspects that arose when she recognized what she had been doing.

- 'Even though I am using sugar to avoid my feelings, I deeply and completely love and accept myself.'
- 'Even though my Mum taught me this and I learned well, I deeply and completely love and accept myself.'
- 'Even though I need sugar to feel better, I deeply and completely love and accept myself.'

Then she continued tapping the points using Reminder Phrases such as:

- 'I need sugar to feel better'
- 'My mum taught me that'
- 'Sugar makes everything better for me'
- 'I have to have sugar to stop feeling'
- 'It is all my Mum's fault'
- 'She wanted me to feel better!'
- 'I need sugar to squash my feelings'
- 'Maybe'
- 'Maybe not!'

Whenever Jane felt a craving coming on she would tap to reduce it and then fire her Heart Anchor. In this way, she did not experience the intense feelings of loss and deprivation she used to feel when she dieted. By using the Heart Anchor in this way she was able to 'fill herself up' with positive feelings and she noticed that her physiology changed at the same time; she no longer felt empty inside.

Then Jane decided to address the issue of losing weight many times but always putting the weight back on – and more. When she revisited the times when she had been her ideal weight she realized there was a common thread, namely that people treated her differently, specifically men. She came in for much more attention and sexual advances and while she wanted a loving relationship somehow it felt unsafe for her. She wanted these men to love her regardless of her shape and looks and all the attention to her body made her very nervous.

She was discovering a huge internal conflict that needed resolving. So she went back to all the times when she had been 'hit' on by men, when she had done things she regretted because she didn't know how to get out of particular situations, when her sexuality had scared her.

When she had cleared this bank of memories and it felt safe to be slim and sexual she realized that she needed to learn some new skills too, specifically how to say no and how to recognize when something didn't feel right to her. She decided to model the behaviour of one of her friends who had very clear boundaries with men and who seemed to be attracting the sort of relationships Jane aspired to. She spoke to her, went out with her, and literally studied how she dealt with over-zealous advances, or pushy men.

Once Jane had cleared those past memories, taken the learnings from them that were useful to her and educated herself in new skill sets she was able to go out and meet guys with a new sense of self-worth, having established her own personal boundaries.

After a few weeks of really focused tapping, persevering even when the temptation to overeat resurfaced, and noticing what triggered that temptation, Jane not only reached her goal weight but she managed to take charge of her eating habits and make her diet more healthy. She was still able to eat her favourite foods, but from a place of control and moderation – and the reality was that she did not want them in the same way anyway, as their purpose had changed. She found that she was naturally drawn to the healthier food groups. She also had much more energy and general *joie de vivre*! Life really was good.

HOW LIFE CHANGED

After working thoroughly and specifically in this way over a relatively short period of time – possibly only a month – Jane succeeded in totally changing her approach to food and to eating. She was able to recognize her feelings and tap to release them as and when she needed to, and she felt happier than she had in many years. A side effect was that she had more energy and lost the excess weight easily. Several months later her weight was still stable and the only complaint was that she had needed to invest in some new clothes as her old ones didn't fit her anymore!

Chapter 9

STOP SMOKING

'Tapping will help you to deal with the cravings associated with smoking, and to break the habits and rituals that are connected to it. At the same time, EFT addresses the underlying anxieties and emotions that lead us to use smoking as a crutch.'

Break habits and rituals

Emotional Freedom Techniques (EFT) can be used to help you stop smoking and it works in several ways. It helps deal with cravings, as well as aiding you to clear feelings about smoking and addressing underlying anxieties and emotions that may have led you to use smoking as a kind of crutch. EFT will also help you break the patterns connected with smoking, such as the times when you smoke, the people you smoke with, the moods and feelings connected to it.

Often the first place to start is with cravings for cigarettes (and for some people, applying the tapping to the craving will be all that is needed to be free from the habit). Different people experience craving in diverse ways. Some people have a strong physical sense of craving, while for others it might be more like a thought or a burst of anxiety. Or perhaps the word 'craving' doesn't really seem to fit the emotion felt and the word 'urge' might work better.

Ask the question

In any case, ask yourself the question: 'How exactly do I feel this craving in my mind and body?' Some people will experience the craving as a tightness in the stomach, perhaps, or a sort of itchiness around their throat and neck. Or maybe you are hearing an internal voice, saying, for example: 'I must have a cigarette... I deserve a cigarette'.

Take your time to think about this so you really tune into your own unique experience. No one else can answer these questions for you. With practice you will become quicker at noticing your own thoughts, feelings and body sensations.

Whatever you identify, it is perfectly okay to go ahead with calling it a 'craving' or an 'urge' because you know what that word signifies for you and the word you choose serves as a useful shorthand for how you feel.

HEART ANCHOR
(See pages 43–45 for more information)

How might you use your Heart Anchor to help you stop smoking?
Consider what emotional state would act as an antidote to smoking for you. For example, you might find the qualities of calmness and optimism helpful. Think of a time when you had that experience, capture the feelings by holding the Heart Anchor as you bring it to mind.

ASK QUESTIONS AND FACE THE ISSUES

• How do I know when to smoke?

_____

• When I want to smoke where do I feel it in my body?

_____

• How exactly do I feel this craving in my mind and body?

_____

UNCOVERING ISSUES

• What emotions am I feeling right now?

_____

• How would I feel if I could never have another cigarette?

_____

DEEPER INTO THE PROCESS

• What does this emotion remind me of?

_____

• When was the first time I felt that?

_____

TESTING

• How much do I need that cigarette now?

_____

• How much do I crave that cigarette now?

_____

Exercise: Stop smoking

Before you begin tapping, assess your craving for a cigarette on the scale of 0–10 (see pages 24–25). Do this quickly because if you are 'in' the craving you need to get tapping straight away. It really is OK to go with the first number, 0–10, that comes into your mind. So let's suppose you decide that the intensity of your craving is 8 on a scale of 0–10. Start tapping immediately, tuning into the physical feeling, the scratchiness in your neck or throat, or however the physical sensation manifests itself for you.

1 Start by repeating three times while tapping the Karate Chop: 'Even though [I have this craving], I deeply and completely love and accept myself.'

2 Follow this by tapping the Tapping Sequence using the Reminder Phrases below on each of the eight points (see pages 20–21). While saying the phrase aloud, tap 5–7 times on each point.

Keep tapping until you feel some sort of shift in the intensity of the craving. Then assess the craving again on your 0–10 scale. Maybe it has gone down from 8 to 5, which is great news.

3 Follow with another Set-Up Statement and continue to repeat three times while tapping the Karate Chop: 'Even though [I still have some of this craving], I deeply and completely love and accept myself.'

4 Next tap the Tapping Sequence using variations on the Reminder Phrases below on each of the eight points as before. While saying the phrase aloud tap 5–7 times on each point.

This craving

This craving

This craving

This intense craving

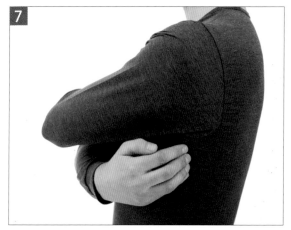
I crave that cigarette

I really crave that cigarette

This craving

I need that cigarette

Beginning of the eyebrow ....*Still some of this craving*

Side of the eye ....*Still some of this craving*

Under the eye......................*This remaining craving*

Under the nose.............................*It hasn't gone yet*

Chin ....*Part of me still wants that cigarette*

Collarbone point ....*This remaining craving*

Under the arm ....*It hasn't gone yet*

Top of the head...................*This remaining craving*

Make sure you adjust the words where you need to in order to reflect your own experience. Again, match your voice with the intensity of the feeling, adjusting as the intensity diminishes.

Take a deep breath at the end of this round and assess the intensity of your cigarette craving again. Supposing your intensity has gone down to somewhere around 3–4 at this stage (and keep tapping until it does), you should ask yourself, 'What emotions am I feeling right now?' All manner of emotions can show up at this stage, but what are they for you? Perhaps you feel anger or sadness. Whatever it is, tap on that feeling next.

5 Pick your phrase, perhaps it is 'Even though I have this feeling of sadness/anger/ frustration, I deeply and completely love and accept myself', then continue tapping on the Karate Chop.

6 Once you feel clear of the craving, or at least more comfortable on your 0–10 scale, ask yourself 'How would I feel if I could never have another cigarette?' This is likely to bring up some fairly deep feelings and emotions – commonly a feeling of deprivation perhaps, or even loss – so begin tapping right away on the Karate Chop with Set-Up Statements and Reminder Phrases based on these feelings. You might choose, for example: 'Even though I feel deprived without that cigarette, I deeply and completely love and accept myself' or 'Even though I really have to have that cigarette, I deeply and completely love and accept myself.'

Match your voice to the intensity of your feeling using for example 'I feel deprived' or variations on this and continue the Tapping Sequence

on each of the eight points (see pages 20–21). Customize the words you use to suit exactly how you are feeling.

When you reach the end of this Tapping Sequence, go back to asking yourself, 'How much do I need that cigarette now? How much do I crave that cigarette now?' to test your work.

If you feel 100 percent clear of the craving at this stage, but can hardly believe it, you could challenge yourself even further. How do you feel when you see an actual cigarette packet? Does any of the craving return at this point? If so, continue to tap to clear it using words such as 'Cigarette packet cravings'. Then, when you are able to see the packet without any craving or other emotional response, try taking out a cigarette. Notice what happens. If you feel any kind of discomfort, continue with your tapping. A final test would be to put the cigarette to your lips, and again if this brings up any intensity continue tapping to clear it using whatever words best describe your feelings.

7 You can follow this Tapping Sequence every time you want to have a cigarette. Rather than tell yourself that you can't have a cigarette, just make a pledge that you will do some tapping first. This is one of the simplest ways to support yourself in stopping smoking. If you do it every time you feel an urge for a cigarette, you will soon begin to find that the times when you want a cigarette become fewer and fewer.

Reclaim your power from the cigarettes.

TOP TAPPING TIPS – STOP SMOKING

FIND YOUR EMERGENCY POINT
Most of us have a point that we find particularly powerful, often the Collarbone point. This is a very useful point to know in an emergency, or in places where you are unable to do the full tapping round.

BE PERSISTENT
EFT does work. Don't give up, there is always a solution, you just haven't found it yet. Ask yourself what holding on to the problem gives you? It can take many sessions to fully clear an entrenched addiction or habit. Human beings are extremely complex, and while some things will change in a couple of tapping rounds, many others will need a lot more attention.

TAP REGULARLY
Make tapping part of your daily routine. How long does it take? Notice any resistance to doing this. Tap on it!

Programme for change
STOP SMOKING
- Begin with cravings – where do I feel this in my body?
- Clear the emotions related to smoking
- Work through your associated memories
- Break patterns – the times, people, places, and moods associated with smoking
- Test the work using the 0–10 scale.

Case study – Tom

Tom is a doctor in his mid thirties who successfully used EFT to stop smoking. Because of his profession, Tom knew all about the dangers of smoking but, despite several attempts, he had not been able to quit.

These repeated 'failures' had damaged his self-esteem and he had started to think that he could never stop and that he could never be happy while he was still smoking. Tom was seemingly stuck in his life; unable to move on, without a relationship, and his attitude towards his career, which had once been his great passion, now seemed to have paled because he had begun to think it was all that he had in his life. He began to feel quite desperate and had lost contact with friends outside his work.

HOW DID HE DO IT?

Tom began working with his cravings in much the same way as we've outlined on pages 120–2. To his surprise, when he asked himself 'How do I experience craving in my mind and body?' he realized that the craving actually came as a surge of joy shooting from his belly to his throat! That was how he knew when to have a cigarette and the craving itself felt good, bringing with it feelings of positive anticipation. He tuned into this physical sensation and began tapping on the Karate Chop point, repeating the Set-Up Statement 'Even though I have this craving, I deeply and completely love and accept myself', three times.

Then he continued tapping, following the Sequence using the phrases 'This craving', 'This surge of joy from my belly to my throat', 'I really want that cigarette', 'I crave that cigarette', and 'I can't wait to have it'.

Tom was 'telling it like it was' and expressing thoughts that he was usually very keen to keep out of his conscious awareness. He had been so busy hating the problem before that he had not been aware of what was actually happening in his

thoughts and feelings that made his smoking seem like a good idea. His experience was that he just found himself smoking again – seemingly against his own will! Telling it like it is and tapping at the same time allowed him to gain a new perspective. It felt like normal sense had been restored and he was able to make a choice whether or not to smoke.

After a couple of rounds the intensity of the initial craving had reduced from 10 to 3. At this point Tom became aware of other emotions emerging. He began to feel angry and the feeling of anger was actually stronger than the desire for the cigarette. Then he had the thought 'but it's my only pleasure'. He realized that cigarettes were a way of rewarding himself and he would feel deprived without them. Employing this realization he altered his Set-Up Statement to 'Even though smoking is my only pleasure, I deeply and completely love and accept myself'.

He tapped the points with Reminder Phrases such as: 'It's my reward', 'It's my friend', 'I would feel deprived without it', I'd be lost without it'.

Then the thought, 'I'd be lonely without it' came to mind, and with it a strong feeling that was a mixture of sadness and loneliness. Tom continued tapping without words as he tuned into this unexpected and intense feeling. As the intensity lessened the feeling crystallized more clearly as a sense of loss, and he felt intuitively that this was really an old feeling trying to get his attention and he asked himself 'What does this feeling of loss remind me of?'

To his surprise the question took him straight to a memory of the time when he had first arrived at medical school. Just before finishing the first term, as he was getting ready to return home, his mother phoned to tell him that the family dog had been put down. He had been devastated by the news and also deeply hurt that his mother hadn't told him for six weeks, thinking that she would 'spare him' from being upset when he had just started university.

Tom was then able to tap through the feelings of anger and resentment that he'd felt towards his mother and he realized that these emotions had kept him from really processing the feelings of loss about his precious dog. Tapping allowed him, for the first time, to release genuine feelings of sadness, loss and betrayal that he had not been able to feel before. He began to feel calmer and more hopeful than he had felt in quite a while. At this point he began to use his Heart Anchor (see pages 43–45), bringing that calmness and hopefulness into it. He also saw what had happened from a new viewpoint, recognizing that his mother's intention was only to protect him, and that she hadn't meant him to feel so hurt. From this place, he found that he was able to forgive her for the decision she had made in what must have been a very difficult situation, and to feel compassion for her.

At this stage Tom had been tapping for about an hour. After this initial piece of work, in the two days that followed, Tom still smoked, but his way of smoking had changed. When he thought of smoking his thoughts were no longer charged with the kind of anxious excitement that he identified in the first session. Now there was a flatness when he thought of smoking, and he tapped on this 'flat craving' as he began to realize that he actually wanted to smoke less and less.

DEEPER INTO THE PROCESS

Encouraged by the progress he'd made, Tom was now in a position to disrupt some of his rituals around smoking. He made a list of all the times he used to smoke, or wanted to smoke, or thought he couldn't do without smoking, and tapped through them. For example, he began tapping on the Karate Chop: 'Even though I have to smoke after a meal/ shift/at a party, I deeply and completely love and accept myself.' Again, telling it like it is while tapping works. In this instance it worked to disrupt the connection between the thought and the action.

After just one week of paying attention to his physical sensations, as well as the thoughts and feelings that told him when to smoke, Tom's cravings began to subside and he no longer had any urge to smoke. He really had emotional freedom and found that he no longer had any need to use his willpower to stay stopped. He tested the work by thinking through and visualizing himself in all the places and with all the people he used to connect with smoking until he found he could think of them all and just feel neutral. Then he tested himself again by actually doing all of those things – going to a party, going home alone after a shift, and so on, knowing that if at any time he felt even a glimmer of the old compulsion he could tap to clear the feelings as soon as he noticed them.

HOW LIFE CHANGED

A year later Tom described himself as happier, healthier and 'in love with life again'. He was thriving, in a relationship and feeling good about the future. With hindsight he realized he had given away his power to cigarettes by believing they were his source of joy. Of course, that had never been his conscious intention, but using EFT had allowed him to see through his own faulty thinking and misguided positive intentions. Interestingly, he also felt that his experience with EFT and smoking made him a better doctor because he understood how so many patients cling on to unhealthy behaviour, seemingly against their own will.

Chapter 10

ATTRACT ABUNDANCE

'Your limiting beliefs are the only obstacle standing in the way of you having the kind of love, money, success, rewards, friendships and fun you really desire. Begin using EFT today to create abundance in your life.'

Abundance as a state of mind

What is abundance? Abundance might be an unfamiliar word to you and many of us rarely use the word because we are often so busy believing life is a struggle, money doesn't grow on trees, people like us don't get rich, and on and on. Abundance is a positive state of mind first, and the ability to manifest good things in our lives follows from that state of mind.

What would you be doing if your success were guaranteed?

Do you want to know what really stands in the way of you having the kind of love, money, success, rewards, friendships and fun you desire? The answer is: only your own limiting beliefs about what is possible for you. You can use EFT to create abundance in your life. First you will need to discover how old, entrenched beliefs may be limiting you today – sometimes in subtle ways.

The best place to start is to ask yourself:

- What do I want? or
- How do I want things to be instead of what I have been experiencing?

The chances are that right now you will probably find it difficult to create an idea in your mind of the you who is able to attract money, qualities and experiences to yourself in just the kind of way you would really like. Close your eyes and try. If you are able to do that in your mind, in full technicolour, with all the sounds and feelings that go with it, then the chances are that you have already created that reality for yourself. What tends to happen is that when we go into our imagination in this way we get all kinds of interference, the picture is fuzzy, intermittent, or just not there. Or we get all manner of what we call 'Yes, buts', which show up in the form of thoughts like: 'Yes but... I am not good enough to have that…' or 'Yes but…I wouldn't like the way people would respond to me if I had X…'

HEART ANCHOR
(See pages 43–45 for more information)

How might you use your Heart Anchor to attract abundance into your life?
What would you like to invite into your life? Vividly imagine yourself having it (you may need to tap to clear any interferences). Keep doing this until you can hold the Heart Anchor and see a consistent picture of the you who already has what you want.

ASK QUESTIONS AND FACE THE ISSUES

• What do I want?

_____

_____

_____

• What would I be doing if my success were guaranteed?

_____

_____

_____

• What do I want things to be like instead of what I have been experiencing?

_____

_____

_____

• When did I first learn 'I am not good enough'?

_____

_____

_____

• What does this remind me of?

_____

_____

_____

Exercise: Attract abundance

The first step is to work out the 'yes buts' for you. And then we can apply the tapping to these particular 'yes buts'. An example might be 'Even though I just don't feel good enough to have exactly what I want in my life, I deeply and completely love and accept myself .' So a complete first round working on an abundance issue might be as follows:

1 Start by repeating the following Set-Up Statement three times while tapping the Karate Chop: 'Even though [I don't feel good enough to have exactly what I want in my life], I deeply and completely love and accept myself.'

2 Follow this by tapping the Tapping Sequence using the Reminder Phrases 'I just don't feel good enough' or variations, 'I can't have what I want', 'Other people can have what they want' or 'I'm not good enough to have what I want in my life' on each of the eight points (see pages 20–21). While saying the phrase aloud, tap 5–7 times on each point.

I just don't feel good enough

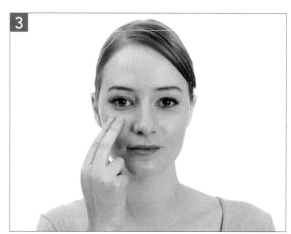

I just don't feel good enough

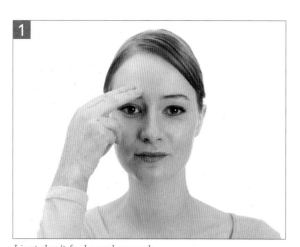

I just don't feel good enough

I can't have what I want

Other people can have what they want

I can't have what I want

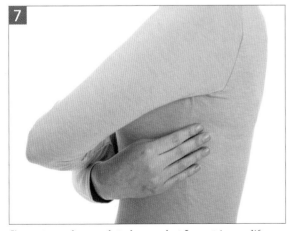

I'm not good enough to have what I want in my life

I just don't feel good enough

Now, the very fact that you are emphasizing this thought, 'I just don't feel good enough', will have set off a kind of internal search. Your brain will be whirring through all the past experiences where you may have learned 'I am not good enough', whether you are consciously aware of this happening or not.

3 So now is a good time to ask yourself the question directly, 'When did I first learn "I am not good enough"?'

The chances are that a particular memory will come to mind. As we are growing up some of us inadvertently learn 'I am not good enough'. Perhaps a particular situation or sequence of events occurred when you felt overwhelmed or out of your depth. When this happens it is very easy to move from thinking 'I don't understand' to 'I am stupid' or 'I am not good enough'. The limiting beliefs we carry around with us in later life are born out of just these kinds of situations. In the end it is not so much what happens to us that matters, as what we decide about ourselves at these critical points in time.

Take pleasure in attracting abundance into your life.

4 When you are able to identify maybe two or three really significant experiences where you may have learned 'I am not good enough', then you have some really worthwhile material to work with using EFT. Now you can clear the interferences to you naturally attracting abundance into your life. Use the Movie Technique (see pages 33–34) whereby you take these two or three memories and give them particular titles that sum up what happened and the emotions around what happened. If you are thinking of a troublesome childhood memory, the title might be something like 'Auntie Sarah Forgot my Birthday'.

5 Rate how you feel right now on the 0–10 scale and then begin tapping using the Set-Up Statement: 'Even though I have this "Auntie Sarah Forgot my Birthday" memory, I deeply and completely love and accept myself.' Repeat this three times while tapping on the Karate Chop and then tap through all the points in the Tapping Sequence saying the Reminder Phrase 'Auntie Sarah Forgot my Birthday'. As you are doing that you can run through the actual details of the memory – just like a movie.

Complete at least one full round before rating the intensity again, and comparing how strongly you felt about this memory before tapping to how you feel about it right now. These kinds of memories get in the way of you attracting abundance to yourself right now, today. Once you have cleared two or three of these significant memories go back to asking yourself:

- How do I want to be?
- Who will I be?
- How will the me who is able to effortlessly attract the things that I want in my life look?

Whether you want to attract financial abundance, find a dream partner or experience more peace and love in your life, the chances are that when you go back and imagine your desired reality again you will be able to get a clearer picture of the you who is able to attract exactly what you want into your life.

The case study on pages 134–7 shows how Robin worked initially on 'seeing himself clearly' with EFT, and then found himself presented with the next piece, and then the next piece, allowing him to make profound changes in his sense of self and in his life.

TOP TAPPING TIPS – ATTRACT ABUNDANCE

WHAT ARE YOUR DREAMS?
Imagine yourself doing what you really want, looking the way you want to look – can you see yourself clearly? Tap to clear any blocks that stand in the way of you seeing yourself, or any unexpected negative responses that surface.

TAP FOR DESERVING ISSUES
'Even though I don't deserve to X…'
'Even though I am not allowed X…'
'Even though I am not good enough for X…'
'Even though people like me don't deserve X…'

TAP FOR BLOCKING BELIEFS AROUND CAPABILITIES
'Even though I can't have that…
'Even though I will never be able to have/do that…'
'Even though I am not capable of X…'

Programme for change

ATTRACT ABUNDANCE

- Ask yourself 'What do I want?': Tap on a daily basis to see the answer to this question clearly
- When you ask 'What do I want?', what are your 'Yes, buts'?
- Clear associated memories that may be interfering with attracting abundance
- Test the intensity of your feelings
- Look out for abundance coming your way!

Tapping on abundance will give you a sense of the power of your own mind to create new possibilities in your life.

Case study – Robin

Robin was a computer engineer, aged 24. Until a friend recommended he visit a hypnotherapist to stop smoking he had never experienced any kind of complementary therapy, psychology or healing.

In fact, he was highly sceptical of 'flakey stuff'! He did, however, follow up his friend's recommendation. He was intrigued because this friend had stopped smoking with such ease after hypnotherapy sessions. Robin badly wanted to stop smoking himself and decided it was worth a shot, but doubted it was possible without a lot of willpower and heartache. He said he wanted to believe in 'the magic wand that waved away all his problems' but didn't think it was very likely to exist.

As it turned out, Robin really did get more than he thought possible. He did stop smoking and the hypnotherapist introduced him to EFT. He became fascinated by how it worked and, having been taught how to use EFT for cigarette cravings, he really credited it with helping ease his passage into a new life as a non-smoker. Tapping seemed to him to be so powerful that he began to wonder what else he might be able to achieve with it.

Robin began to search for ideas and information on the Internet and came across the Heart Anchor (see pages 43–45). He began using it straight away, loving it, and going out of his way to find things to appreciate. He began to see the world through different eyes and to feel quite different himself.

It was a very exciting time for Robin. At around the same time he came across an article on using EFT to attract abundance into your life. It was certainly a new concept for him, and even as he was feeling unsure about it, he also felt a little bit intrigued and drawn to the idea.

After three months without smoking, Robin noticed in himself a growing desire to expand his horizons. He wasn't really sure how to go about it, yet – he just knew that he was beginning to have a sense of the power of his own mind to create new possibilities in his life.

He had been working with the Heart Anchor for a few weeks and it seemed to have opened up new ways of thinking for him. Robin began to think about what he would like to have in his life – who he would like to be in the world now. He also began thinking that he had never had 'a proper girlfriend'. In fact he had always avoided such matters. Now, he decided, it was time for an experiment.

HOW DID HE DO IT?

First of all Robin asked himself, 'How do I see myself now?' The honest answer was that he currently thought of himself as nerdy, dull and comfortable hiding away, yet with a good sense of humour, and decent looking. Next he asked himself, 'How would I like to see myself instead?' He wanted to see himself as attractive, strong, fun and engaged with other people and the world around him.

Next, Robin closed his eyes and tried to imagine himself in the way he wanted. At first he just couldn't do it. What came to his mind made him cringe – he saw himself as someone dull, dark, featureless and old. He couldn't see his face clearly, and if he did manage to focus on his face his body disappeared. He began to tap repeating the following Set-Up Statements three times while tapping the Karate Chop:

- 'Even though I can't see myself clearly, I deeply and completely love and accept myself'.

- 'Even though I can't see myself as I want to be, I deeply and completely love and accept myself'.
- 'Even though I just can't see clearly yet, I deeply and completely love and accept myself'.

He followed the Set-Up Statement by tapping around the eight Tapping Sequence points and repeating the following Reminder Phrases:

- 'Can't see myself clearly as I want to be'
- 'Can't see myself as I want to be…yet'
- 'Can't see myself'
- 'Can't see myself clearly.'

Robin closed his eyes and checked the picture again after a couple of rounds. It was beginning to get clearer, although there was still more to do. He adjusted the Set-Up as follows and continued:

- 'Even though I still can't see myself clearly as I want to be, I deeply and completely love and accept myself.'

Also adjusting the Reminder Phrase to:

- 'Still can't see myself clearly'
- 'Still can't quite see myself as I want to be.'

After a few rounds Robin was able to consistently hold a picture in his mind of himself as he wanted to be. The next challenge he set himself, however, was to 'see' the girl of his dreams. At first this proved impossible. He could see himself, but not himself with a girl.

However, at about this time he did notice one change in himself in everyday life. Previously whenever he had seen an attractive girl in the street or anywhere else, he had always looked away, thinking she would never be interested in him. Now, since he was actively looking out for all kinds of positive qualities to add to his Heart Anchor, he was finding beautiful things to appreciate all around him, including attractive girls.

Robin persisted with his tapping. He did have the occasional twinge when he thought how weird his work colleagues would consider his behaviour if they knew what he was doing, but on the whole he was really enjoying his secret experiment. He was having more fun than he had done in a long time.

After a while, when he tried again to 'see' the image that he wanted of himself – happy and content with his girlfriend, to his great pleasure he began to be able to get the picture in focus.

DEEPER INTO THE PROCESS

The next stage of Robin's experiment brought up a very interesting 'Yes, but…' that could have derailed his progress but actually turned out to be an opportunity for major change. Now that he was able to picture himself and his girl, he thought he would try to imagine asking her out. Instantly he had feelings of near panic, and a loud voice in his head would shout: 'DON'T ASK!'

Feeling surprised and shaken, he asked himself, 'Where did that come from?' The answer took him straight to an old memory. He remembered himself as a five-year-old boy innocently asking an attractive young teacher home for tea. She had responded by shouting: 'DON'T ASK!' right in his face. The memory had come and gone in a flash but was very vivid – he saw very clearly the expression on her face and heard the tone of her voice.

Robin was able to make a movie in his mind of the memory. It was really just a vivid, still picture capturing his teacher's face and tone. Robin began tapping: 'Even though I have this "Don't Ask!" movie, I deeply and completely love and accept myself.' The intensity of his feelings related to this incident quickly dropped from a full 10 down to about 5, and then more insights and new perspectives started to come through.

The thought occurred to Robin that he had found his teacher so attractive, and yet her face and voice had seemed so ugly. He tapped through this and all the aspects that came to him, moving quickly and feeling no need to pause to do Set-Up Statements for each thought. He used the following statements:

- 'That ugly voice'
- 'The tone of her voice'
- 'Her awful expression'
- 'The shock'
- 'I thought she was pretty and then she did that'
- 'I loved her and then she did that'
- 'She hurt me'
- 'She really hurt me.'

Through this process, Robin was telling it like it is (as his five-year-old self).

At this point, compassion for the younger Robin began to come through. Robin wished he could have been there to help the little boy who didn't understand what he had done wrong. He moved from anger at the teacher to compassion for her, and whatever had been going on for her to make her react in the way she did. At this point he touched his Heart Anchor and sent love to everyone involved in the incident. Suddenly he felt very peaceful.

After this, Robin thought about how, as a teenager, he had been afraid of talking to girls and had never asked anyone for a date. His fear made sense to him now, in the light of the memory he'd unearthed. He also had the deeper realization that his fear was based on the mistaken judgement of a five-year-old boy, not the young man he was today.

Now he found he could hold his Heart Anchor and see a consistent picture of himself with his dream girl. In fact, he realized he had actually jumped a few stages beyond just asking her out. He was seeing himself already in a loving, fun relationship!

HOW LIFE CHANGED

It wasn't long before Robin found love in real life. One day, at work, he spotted a 'new' girl. He thought she must have joined one of the other companies that shared the building with his own. He asked her for a date (without a qualm). As it turned out, she had been in her job for two years and had all the while been admiring Robin from afar. He just hadn't been able to 'see' her.

AUTHORS' COMMENT

Robin's case study beautifully demonstrates several very important points.

1. The mindset of possibility

Notice how, once Robin was free from his old problem of smoking, his mind started to consider new possibilities. Attachment to problem states interferes with our natural creativity. Once Robin had succeeded in giving up smoking, he automatically assumed a mindset of possibility.

2. The importance of visualization

Visualization creates the blueprint for whatever we want to attract into our lives. However, many of us are convinced that we can't do it. Everyone has the capacity to visualize – it's a natural ability. Here Robin skilfully uses EFT to remove the interferences to 'seeing clearly'. He begins by working on seeing himself clearly, then moves on to the greater challenge of seeing himself with a girl.

3. 'Yes, buts…' are opportunities!

Robin's experiment is potentially derailed when he tries to imagine himself asking his girl out. However, he seizes the opportunity to clear the impact an old memory has had on his life once it presents itself. He runs quickly through a whole series of aspects related to the memory without stopping to do Set-Up Statements for each one.

Chapter 11

TROUBLESHOOTING, SELF-ENQUIRY & FAQS

'Those who get the best results from EFT approach it in a spirit of curiosity about themselves, exploring any blocks from a place of enquiry and possibility.'

Troubleshooting

While EFT is simple to use and relatively trouble-free, there may be times when you get stuck and need to be more creative in your work. In this chapter there is a list of useful questions that are designed to help you get past your blocks. The questions are by no means exhaustive, and we encourage you to become curious about your individual process and to explore any blocks from a place of enquiry and possibility.

Stuckness is simply a form of subconscious resistance often created by issues around safety, deserving, fear and desire. We call these 'Primary Reversals', and they are simply more creative ways of being psychologically reversed.

Primary Reversals happen when, in some way, usually subconsciously, we feel that releasing a particular problem is not OK for us. These are the ways in which we trap ourselves and can find ourselves going around in circles. Don't worry, this is very common and the solution is easy! Just ask yourself some of the questions below and notice your response, both physically and emotionally.

It is often simpler to begin working with any physical sensations that you experience as these are a direct communication from the subconscious, whereas we are skilled at ignoring our conscious thoughts. If you notice any physiological sensations of any sort, this is your place to begin tapping. Or, if you get a strong emotional response, then start there, using the techniques you are now familiar with from having read this book.

For example:
- 'Even though I don't deserve to get over this I deeply and completely love and accept myself.'
- 'Even though they don't deserve for me to get over this I deeply and completely love and accept myself.'
- 'Even though it is not safe for me to get over this I deeply and completely love and accept myself.'
- 'Even though it is not safe for others if I get over this I deeply and completely love and accept myself.'
- 'Even though I am frightened to get over this I deeply and completely love and accept myself.'
- 'Even though I don't want to get over this I deeply and completely love and accept myself.'

OK, so we know you DO want to get over the problem you are dealing with, but try tapping using these statements anyway, and you may be surprised to discover that there is a part of you that feels differently! This is often apparent with weight-loss issues, and can be connected with feelings of deprivation: 'I will be deprived if I get over this'; 'I won't be able to eat my favourite foods, have my treats', and so on.

QUESTIONS FOR SELF-ENQUIRY

- When did it (the problem) first start?

_____

- What was happening in your life at that time?

_____

- How do you feel about it now?

_____

- How would you like to feel instead?

_____

- What would you like instead?

_____

- If there was a deeper emotion underlying this problem, what might it be?

_____

- What memory would you rather not have?

_____

- If you had to teach someone else to do what you do, how would you do it?

_____

- If that feeling had a voice, what would it say?

_____

- Who/what/when/where specifically?

_____

- What did that experience mean about you?

_____

- What do you wish you had never done?

_____

- What is stopping you having what you want in your life now?

_____

- What would happen if this problem wasn't there anymore?

_____

- What happens when you think that thought on a physical level?

_____

- What happens when you think that thought on an emotional level?

_____

- If there were an emotional contributor to this pain, what might it be?

_____

- What does that remind you of?

_____

- Where in your body do you feel it?

_____

- When was the first time/worst time you can remember feeling the same kind of feeling?

_____

- What decisions did you make about yourself at that time (the time of a specific negative memory)?

_____

- What decisions did you make about the world at that time (the time of a specific negative memory)?

_____

- If you could live your life over again, what person or event would you prefer to leave out?

_____

Become curious about your individual process and explore any blocks from a place of enquiry and possibility.

TRIED AND TESTED WAYS TO BURST THROUGH BEING STUCK

- Drink a big glass of water
- Tap on being stuck 'Even though I am stuck I deeply and completely love and accept myself'
- Shout the Set-Up Statement
- Vary your voice tone around the points
- Say it as though you mean it
- Change your words
- Introduce words such as maybe, possibly, perhaps to soften the positive affirmation
- Check you are being specific enough in your language

FAQs

What does EFT stand for?

Emotional Freedom Techniques.

How long has EFT existed?

Gary Craig, the founder of EFT, developed it in its current form in the mid 1990s in the US.

Do I always have to say the words out loud?

Yes, ideally you should, or at least to begin with. We find that speaking the words out loud while tapping is the most effective approach, but there will be times when this is not possible. At those times it is fine to say the words in your head. Once you have learned the tapping points, your subconscious will be able to respond well even when you can only think the words.

I am not good with numbers; do I have to use the 0–10 scale?

No, you can use your arms to measure the level of intensity of your feelings. This is especially useful when tapping with children.

How many times should I tap on each point?

As a rule, between 5 and 7 times is plenty, but more will not do any harm. We suggest tapping as many times as fits the rhythm of the words you are saying on each point.

How fast should I tap?

This will vary according to the 'energy' of the problem you are working with. For example, tapping on anger may require a faster tapping touch than tapping on sadness. Experiment on yourself until you get a sense of what feels right for you. There is no right or wrong, you are merely sending a vibration along each point.

How hard should I tap?

Tap hard enough to feel it, but not so hard that you hurt yourself! You will probably find that your tapping varies according to the issue you are addressing.

What happens if I miss out a point?

It does not seem to make any difference. However, when you notice, bring the point back into the next round.

What happens if I get the order of the points wrong?

Nothing, they are only illustrated in a particular order to make them easier to remember.

How do I find the right words to use?

The first and only rule is to make sure your words specifically match the issue you are working with. Other than that, they are your words and you can't get them wrong! If you get stuck at any point, go back to the words you are using and play around with them seeing whether something else resonates more strongly for you. If it does, change your words accordingly.

How do I know when to stop?

Stop when you have successfully lowered the intensity of feeling around the issue you are working with. Also you should stop when the issue or the tapping just seem boring.

Which side of the body should I tap?

You can tap on either side as the meridians are mirrored on both sides of the body like inkblots. In fact, you can also tap double-handed going down both sides of the body at the same time. This is a useful trick if the intensity of your feelings suddenly becomes very strong.

Which hand should I use?

Usually it is best to use your dominant hand as this tends to be more comfortable.

Is it OK to cry?

Tears are one of nature's release mechanisms and it is fine to cry while you tap. Just keep tapping – you will work through and release the feelings quickly. If you are right 'in' the emotion then there is no need to say any words.

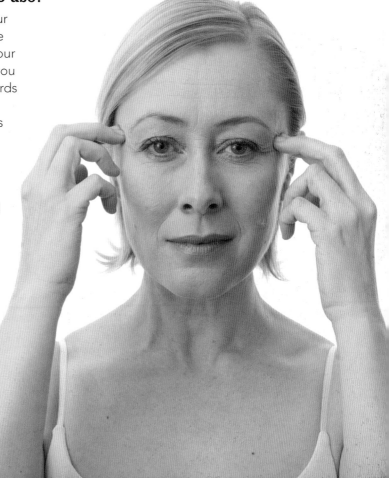

Is EFT safe for children?

Yes, and they love it. You can teach very young children how to tap. It is often helpful to let them tap on their favourite toy. Obviously you will need to adjust the Set-Up Statements accordingly, possibly using phrases such as 'I am cool' or 'Mum loves me' instead of 'I deeply and completely love and accept myself'. Small children love the idea of having their own 'magic buttons'! Children of all ages, from tiny to teenagers, use tapping and find it a fun and useful way to deal with everyday life events that, left untreated, can result in the distorted belief systems we have discussed earlier in this book. Some schools now teach tapping as an afterschool club.

Will tapping make things worse?

No, although it may seem like it in the short term. Sometimes, when you clear one layer of emotion, another deeper layer that may seem more intense comes to the surface. It is important to take time to really look at that layer in order to recognize that it is a different piece to the bit you were tapping on before. You will have uncovered a new, deeper aspect of the original problem and that, ultimately, is a very positive thing, although it may feel a little uncomfortable initially. The trick is to KEEP TAPPING! The feelings you experience will subside and you will have done a very important piece of healing.

Will the results last?

Usually, yes – as long as you have uncovered all the aspects connected to the issue. For example, you may have been working on a fear of flying and tapped on the thoughts or memories of take-off and landing, but perhaps you've forgotten about your anxiety surrounding turbulence. Then if you are on a flight and it hits some turbulence, the fear might seem to return. In fact, this won't be the case – all that you would need to do would be to tap on the aspect of turbulence that you have overlooked and it will clear fully.

Why do I always have to tap on the negative? Isn't this just another way of reinforcing it?

No. With Emotional Freedom Techniques we are directly treating the effects of our negative thoughts, feelings and behaviours – it is these effects that contribute to our general dis-ease, whether it be physical or emotional.

When we tap to release the energetic charge of the negative issues, the positives rise naturally to the surface as a result. All we need to do is to clear the space to allow them to do so, as 'positive' is our default way of being, however unlikely that may seem to you right now. Once we have begun to clear our negative thoughts, feelings and behaviours we can introduce some new ways of working, such as with the Heart Anchor (see pages 43–45), to further enhance and reinforce our positive well-being. But we have to clear away the negatives first, to make space.

Can I tap while taking medication?

While there is no evidence to suggest that there is a problem with tapping while taking medication, and we have worked with many people on medication ranging from the contraceptive pill to chemotherapy, if you have any doubts, we recommend that you seek advice from your medical practitioner before beginning to tap.

Is it safe to tap during pregnancy?

Yes.

What should I do when tapping doesn't work?

Refer to the troubleshooting tips located on pages 140–4.

Can I tap on behalf of someone else?

While there is evidence of the efficacy of surrogate tapping we do not recommend tapping for someone else as you learn. However, you can certainly tap on your need to change others, however positive your intention might be! You can also tap with another person (see page 28).

What if I can't remember much of my childhood?

Just begin where you are now and don't worry about it. The chances are that memories will show up as you clear your issues in the here and now, but if they don't it is not a problem. Another possibility is to use your imagination to create a fictional scenario and tap in the same way that you would for a real memory using the Movie Technique (see pages 33–34). Interestingly, this can work equally well to produce positive results. Check in on how you feel in your body as you tell the fictional story to yourself and tap on any physiological discomfort that you feel as you go through it.

THE NEXT STEP

'Mastering tapping can take you from problem-solving to personal transformation. Once you make the decision to begin, previously fixed limitations about who you are and what you are capable of melt away. Who knows what you can achieve next?'

A final word

Congratulations on making it this far in your journey with EFT. We hope you are already reaping the benefits of this wonderful healing technique. As with learning any new skill, practice is essential. Once you get started you will soon discover the subtleties of this amazing tool and how it can work best for you.

You will quickly come to have a closer relationship with your own mind/body system and understand how the two interact to create the reality that you experience today. You will also learn how to use the tapping skills to create the reality that you really want, not a compromise. You are already your own self-expert – although you may not realize it yet – and hopefully this book will provide you with a personal user manual.

You may surprise yourself as you work through the chapters of this book and bring tapping into your world. You may discover that change doesn't have to be difficult or take a long time, and that it can even be fun! One of the great benefits of EFT is that you can apply it to yourself to make profound and lasting changes.

However, there may be times when you come up against blocks in your self-work with tapping, in spite of persistence and your best attempts at troubleshooting. These are the times when it can be useful to see an experienced and creative EFT practitioner for a session or two to clear any subconscious saboteurs that may be obstructing your progress. You will find more information on locating a suitable EFT practitioner in the Further Training and Resources section of this book (see pages 152–153).

If you have been bitten by the EFT bug and are keen to discover more, you will find that there are many opportunities for further learning. There is a wealth of information available on the Internet, and a lot of it is free or low cost. There are also accredited professional trainings available, and a host of personal development workshops, practice groups and online forums. It can seem daunting to have to navigate your way through so much information to find what is truly valuable; again, the Further Training and Resources section at the back of this book offers a selection of the best and most useful information available today.

Perhaps you will simply be content to use what you have learned from this book to make changes in your own life, and that is fine too – not everyone wants to continue their education in a formal sense. We truly believe that each and every bit of tapping clears the way to a kinder, safer and more compassionate world. Harnessing the energy of the heart in our lives and in our interactions with others benefits not just ourselves, but also makes a positive and powerful contribution to world peace and joy. So many times we have heard students exclaim: 'Imagine if this were taught in schools!' or 'How come they don't teach you this stuff at school?' Well, coming some day very soon…

For now, you might like to ponder your own, personal contribution. May that be the quiet certainty and strength that exudes from one who has reached a degree of self-acceptance in their own private way, or the thrill of fulfilling your ambitions in a more public way? Once you master tapping as a tool for personal transformation, previously fixed limitations about who you are and what you are capable of will melt away. That, quite simply, is the promise offered by this book.

Finally, we are delighted you have read our book, and thank you for taking the time to do so. Keep coming back to it – you will find that you discover new insights and depths as your inner world changes. Now you have begun the process with a thorough grounding in tapping and the infinite possibilities it offers, who knows how far you can go? We would love you to let us know how you get on with your tapping journey. Above all, have fun with your new skills!

Sue Beer and Emma Roberts
theeftcentre@googlemail.com

Use your new tapping skills to create the reality that you really want.

Further training & resources

EFT INTRODUCTORY WORKSHOP AND PRACTITIONER TRAININGS

AAMET (Association for the Advancement of Meridian Energy Techniques) Certified Trainings at 3 Levels: Introductory, Practitioner and Advanced with Sue Beer and Emma Roberts: www.theeftcentre.com

DIPLOMA IN INTEGRATED ENERGY TECHNIQUES AND NLP (NEURO LINGUISTIC PROGRAMMING) CERTIFICATION

Find out more about the Diploma in Integrated Energy Techniques with Sue Beer and Emma Roberts: www.theeftcentre.com

'OPENING TO LOVE', 'HEALING THE ADDICTED HEART' AND OTHER SPECIALIST WORKSHOPS

For more information about specialist workshops with Sue Beer and Emma Roberts: www.theeftcentre.com

INDIVIDUAL SESSIONS WITH SUE BEER AND EMMA ROBERTS AND EFT CENTRE RECOMMENDED PRACTITIONERS:
www.theeftcentre.com

RECOMMENDED TRAININGS WITH OTHER EFT MASTERS

www.professionaleft.com

Carol Look, EFT Master
www.attractingabundance.com

www.eftmasterslive.com

www.eftmastersworldwide.com

Matrix Reimprinting (Karl Dawson and Sasha Allenby):
www.matrixreimprinting.com

Inner State Repatterning (Tania Prince):
www.eft-courses.co.uk

Simple Energy Techniques
(Steve Wells and Dr David Lake):
www.eftdownunder.com

OTHER RECOMMENDED RESOURCES

AAMET (Association for the Advancement of Meridian Energy Techniques)
www.aamet.com

www.eftuniverse.com

EFT Hub
www.efthub.com

Gary Craig's website
www.emofree.com

ACEP (Association for Comprehensive Energy Psychology) www.acep.org

RECOMMENDED READING

The following books, in particular, will support your learning with EFT and Energy Psychology:

Sue Beer, *Healing the Addicted Heart: 5 Stages of Transformation*. The EFT Centre, 2010.

Emma Roberts, *Even Though I Have Cancer…* The EFT Centre, 2010.

Dawson Church, *The Genie in Your Genes*. Energy Psychology Press, 2009.

Karl Dawson and Sasha Allenby, *Matrix Reimprinting*. Hay House, 2010.

David Feinstein, Donna Eden & Gary Craig, *The Healing Power of EFT and Energy Psychology*. Piatkus, 2006.

Dr Robin Kelly, *The Human Antenna – Reading the Language of the Universe in the Songs of Our Cells*. Energy Psychology Press, 2008.

Dr Robin Kelly, *The Human Hologram: Living Your Life in Harmony with the Unified Field*. Energy Psychology Press, 2011.

Bruce Lipton, *The Biology of Belief*. Mountain of Love/Elite Books, 2005.

Steve Wells & Dr David Lake, *Enjoy Emotional Freedom: Simple Techniques for Living Life to the Full*. Exisle Publishing, 2010.

Doc Childre, *The Heartmath Solution*. Piatkus Books, 1999.

ABOUT THE AUTHORS

Sue Beer and **Emma Roberts** are the co-founders of The EFT Centre. They were two of the first ten practitioners in the world to be awarded the title 'EFT Master' by Gary Craig, founder of EFT.

Sue and Emma are international trainers, presenters and writers. They both have private practices in London, UK, which specialize in using EFT to help people change and find meaning in their lives.

They have worked together for many years and are renowned for the strength of their working relationship, and their skill at introducing seemingly complex ideas with clarity and simplicity. They are passionate about their work and are well known for their ability to initiate profound change in an atmosphere of fun, lightness and love.

Sue is the author of *Healing the Addicted Heart: 5 Stages of Transformation*. Emma is the author of *Even Though I Have Cancer…*.

www.theeftcentre.com

YOUR NOTES

Index

Acknowledgements

AUTHORS' ACKNOWLEDGEMENTS

Thank you to Liz Dean, Leanne Bryan and all the team at Octopus Publishing Group for your gentle guidance and support.

Thank you to Gary Craig for the gift of EFT, for inspiring us and for some wonderful shared experiences.

Above all, thank you to our colleagues, students, clients and friends for sharing our EFT journey; we are still travelling!

PUBLISHERS' ACKNOWLEDGEMENTS

The publishers would like to thank Pauline Bache, Leanne Bryan, Marco Cavallaro, Julia Gray, Mark Kan, Melanie Libird, Jamie Mason, Polly Roberts and Catherine Roney for being such wonderful models. Special thanks go to Julia Gray, who appears on the book's cover.

SPECIAL PHOTOGRAPHY

Copyright © Octopus Publishing Group Limited/Adrian Pope

OTHER PHOTOGRAPHY

Fotolia/nfsphoto 69; /vlorzor 134.

Getty Images/AE Pictures Inc. 58; /Phil Ashley 107; /Newton Daly 32; /Digital Zoo 55; /Hybrid Images 112; /i love images 123; /Janet Kimber 46; /Howard Kingsnorth 132; /Photo and Co. 35; /Jeff Rotman 38; /Sadahito Mori 42; /Shioguchi 36; /STOCK4B/Daniel Reiter 143; /Jacqueline Veissid 72; /Steve West 81.

istockphoto.com/7io 52 (used throughout); / hillwoman2 53 (used throughout).

Consultant Commissioner Liz Dean
Senior Editor Leanne Bryan
Executive Art Editor Juliette Norsworthy
Designer Lizzie Ballantyne
Illustrator Jaz Bahra
Photographer Adrian Pope
Picture Researcher Jennifer Veall
Senior Production Controller Caroline Alberti